D1460047

FLESH & BLOOD

W. Melvin Adams and Vatha Pheng

Based on the experiences of the
Pheng family and others

AUTUMN

HOUSE

AUTUMN HOUSE® PUBLISHING COMPANY

P.O. Box 1139, Hagerstown, Maryland 21741-1139

The author assumes full responsibility for the accuracy of all facts and quotations as cited in this book.

This book was
Edited by Richard W. Coffen
Designed by Bill Kirstein
Cover Design and Illustration: Byron Steele
Type set: 11/12 Sabon

PRINTED IN U.S.A.

96 95 94 93 92 91   10 9 8 7 6 5 4 3 2 1

Library of Congress Cataloging in Publication Data

Adams, W. Melvin.
  Flesh and blood / W. Melvin Adams and Vatha Pheng.
    p.   cm.
    *Based on the experiences of the Pheng family and others."
    1. Pheng, Vatha. 2. Cambodia—Politics and government—1975–
3. Refugees, Political—Cambodia—Biography. 4. Refugees, Political—
United States—Biography. I. Pheng, Vatha. II. Title.
DS554.83.P48A33 1991
956.604'092—dc20
[B]   91-10068
                                             CIP

ISBN 1-878951-15-7

Contents

Preface

For years the eyes of the world focused on the Far East, where the United States armed forces were mired in the jungles of Vietnam. Later they watched as the American government frantically worked at bringing the GI's home. During this emotional time of national confusion and confrontation, another tragedy was unfolding in Missouri-sized Cambodia, just across the Vietnamese border. This heartbreaking event produced very few headlines compared to the Vietnamese coverage. For Americans, Vietnam was on center stage, whereas Cambodia was hidden in the wings. But when the curtain was finally pulled aside and the world's gaze fell upon the ancient nation of Cambodia, between one and two million of its seven million citizens had been killed by one means or another. The death of one million five hundred thousand Cambodians is more than 21 percent of the former population. If the United States lost 21 percent of its population, about 51 million people would die.

Before 1981 I was vaguely aware of Cambodia's existence. In my travels I had visited Vietnam during the war and had also traveled in Thailand. But it was never my privilege to visit Cambodia, nor had I met any of its people. This all changed when a local church asked me to assist Cambodian refugees arriving in the Washington, D.C. area.

Several years later, Vatha Pheng, a refugee, mentioned to me that she had written about one of her experiences. The story she related on these few pages shocked me. Later, Vatha and her family told me the full story of their enslavement and escape. With their permission, I tape recorded their stories. At times voices quivered and tears sneaked down their cheeks as they divulged their experiences during those disastrous 55 months of agony and death.

Later I had the opportunity to visit Cambodia, now known as Kampuchea. Some of the scars of the holocaust are still visible in both the landscape and the people.

This book relates the true story of the Pheng family. Since Vatha was the one who first inspired the writing and has been the chief spokesman for her family, it is her story. Her mother, Leang Kim Tan, her two sisters, Letine and *By*, and her two brothers, Lim and Leang, assisted her. Here and there I have included additional information that I have culled from others. But this story is *not* fiction. It remains the true account of the Pheng family's terrible ordeal.

Also assisting, by reading drafts and making suggestions, were Letine, *By*, my son Willis, my niece Marcia, friends Janice Miller and Jim Buie, and my daughter, Berneva. My one daily supporter has been my wife, Olive, who has been more than patient during the time I spent on the story. Her support and encouragement has been very much appreciated.

The dates found in the story are general periods except where a specific date is noted. Distances are approximate. The pictures were either taken by me or with my camera at my request.

After hearing this compelling story and learning of the events surrounding it, I understand why Cambodians fled to my country. Also it has given me a new appreciation of these people and their love of freedom. For this I am grateful to Vatha and her family.

—Melvin Adams

Getting Acquainted

An overall view of the Pheng family will help in sorting out the names. The spouses and grandchildren are included. The 10 children are listed in the order of their age.

Mr. Huot Eng Pheng	Father
Mrs. Leang Kim Tan	Mother
Sour Ly	Daughter
Bun Thuon Lok	Son-in-law
Seila	Grandson
(Name unknown)	Granddaughter
Nakry	Daughter
Mong Hin	Son-in-law
Patrick Roux	Son-in-law
Prasith	Grandson
Visal	Grandson
Joel	Grandson
Leng	Son
By	Daughter
Sokhom Phann	Son-in-law
Annong	Granddaughter
Anname	Granddaughter
Letine	Daughter
Vatha	Daughter
Saat	Son
Sarith	Son
Mom	Daughter-in-law
Renee	Granddaughter
Ishmael	Grandson
Lim	Son
Leang	Son

Guide to Pronunciation of Cambodian Words

The Khmer (Cambodian) language is uninflected (Chinese, for instance, is an inflected language—the same word can mean different things, depending on the rise and fall of the voice during pronunciation), and, like English, is alphabetic (the Chinese language is not alphabetic but has a single character or picture-word that denotes each word). Khmer has 22 vowels and 36 consonants. It is written with a form of Sanskrit script. Most Khmer words are of one to three syllables.

Because of the wide variety of sounds (phonemes) in the Khmer language, the pronunciation guides that follow are only approximations. Some of the spoken sounds are practically undetectable to American ears. Instead of using diacritical marks, which most of us find confusing, we have resorted to using words or combinations of letters that will generally be regarded, we hope, as self-evident (some letters in the words remain silent or are barely pronounced). We have put in all upper case (CAPITAL) letters the part of the syllable that receives the most emphasis (though Khmer has syllables that receive either major or minor emphasis): for example, TELeVISion or we would give the following as the guide: TELLuhVIZHun. Some syllables are run together quickly; in such instances, we have *not* separated the syllables with a hyphen.

Word(s)	Guide	Definition
Andong Cheng	ON-DONG CHANG	Name of a village
Angkor Wat	ANGKor waht	Ruins of large, ancient temple
Annong	AHNong	*By's* older daughter
Anname	AHname	*By's* younger daughter
Apsara	AHPsahRAH	From Hindu myth
Battambang	Baht-DAHMbong	Second largest city in Cambodia (Kampuchea)
Bonzes	Bones	Buddhist monk
Bun Thuon Lok	BUN twahn LOCK	Sour Ly's husband
By	Bee	Vatha's older sister; because the reader might confuse the name with the English preposition "by," this proper name will be italicized throughout the book

Word(s)	Guide	Definition
Chee	Chee	Cambodian measure of ⅛ ounce of gold
Chhoeu Sattek	CHOeuh sah-TAY	"Memory sickness"
Chhlang Tonle	Chlong TonLAY	Crossed the river
Chlops	Chlahps	Spies
Choeung Ek	Chyung Ik	Official name of "Killing Fields;" literally means "champions"
Chong Chhdor	Chong ChhDOR	Village
Chon Buri	Chawn bo-REE	Name of a refugee camp in Thailand
Dang Rek	Dong Rak	Range of mountains between Thailand and Cambodia (Kampuchea)
Deuch	Dewtch	Leader of the Khmer Rouge secret police
Eng	Ang	Vatha's uncle
Gautama	Gaw-TAHM-ah	Founder of Buddhism
Huot Eng Pheng	Hoo oht Ang Pang	Vatha's father
Joel	Joe-AL	Nakry's youngest son
Kampuchea	GKAHM-poo-CHEEah	Khmer Rouge (and now official) name for Cambodia
Kampong Chhnang	Gkahm-PONG Chnang	Name of town
Khao I Dang	Cow ee dung	Name of a refugee camp in Thailand
Katha	GkahTAH	Cambodian charm or amulet
Khmer Rouge	K MARE rouzhe	Communist party in Cambodia
Koki	Gkoh-GKEE	Tree
Nokorbal	No-gkor-BAWL	Khmer Rouge secret police
Konpong Thom	GKAWN-pong TOM	Name of village
Kosang	Gkah-SAHNG	Constructive criticism
La Press	Lah Press	French newspaper in Phnom Penh
Le Phnom	La pnawm	Name of a hotel in Phnom Penh

Word(s)	Guide	Definition
Leang	LEEang	Vatha's youngest brother
Leang Kim Tan	LEEang kim tahn	Vatha's mother's maiden name
Leng	Lang	Vatha's older brother
Letine	LehtTEEN	Vatha's older sister
Lim	Lim	Vatha's younger brother
Lon Nol	Lawn NALL	Former president of Cambodia
Lumphini	Lom-PEE-nee	Transit refugee camp
Meatophoum	MEEit-toh-POOM	Cambodian newspaper
Mekong	MaKONG	Name of a river
Mong Hin	Mong HIN	Nakry's first husband
Mong Russei	Mong Russay	Name of village
Monivong	Mo-NEE-vong	Name of Boulevard
Mom	Mum	Sarith's wife
Nakry	NA-kree	Vatha's older sister
Neary	NEER-ree	Unmarried young women
Norodom Siha-nouk	Noh-roh-DOM SEE-ha-nuke	Former prince of Cambodia; in Khmer the order of the names are reversed—Sihanouk Norodom
Otaki	Oh-TAH-kee	Name of a village
Patrick Roux	Patrick Roo	Nakry's second husband
Pol Pot	Pawl Pot	Leader of the Khmer Rouge
Phnom Penh	P-nawm Pen	Capital and largest city of Cambodia (Kampuchea)
Phnom Touch	P-nawm Toh(ch)	Large village
Pochentong	Poh-chan-TONG	Airport in Phnom Penh
Preah Vihear	PREEah veh-HEER	Old temple ruins
Prasith	Prah-SIT	Name of village
Pursat	POHsat	Name of village
Renee	RehNAY	Sarith's daughter
Riels	Reel(s)	Cambodian dollar
Saat	Sah-AHT	Vatha's younger brother
Samnak	SAHMnahk	A resting place by the road
Sarith	SahRIT	Vatha's younger brother
Satrei	SatTRAY	Married women

Word(s)	Guide	Definition
Seila	SAYlah	Vatha's nephew (Sour Ly's son)
Siem Reap	SEE-em REE-ap	Name of a town
Sisophon	SEE-so-pon	Name of village
Sleng	Slang	Seed containing quinine-like substance
Stung Treng	Stung Trang	Name of province
Sarong	Sa-RONG	Ladies' long skirt
Sokhom Phann	So-KUM Pun	By's husband
Sour Ly	Soor Lee	Vatha's oldest sister
Tuol Sleng	TWO-ohl slang	Vatha's high school
Tonle Sap	Tun-LAY sap	Name of river and lake
Vatha	Wah-TAH	Co-author
Veal Treng	Veel trang	Name of village
Visal	Vee-SAHL	Nakry's son
Yotear	YOH-teer	Khmer Rouge word for soldier(s)

Thursday, April 17, 1975

Father—Huot Eng Pheng—and his family were all at home. With so many rockets exploding in the city, it was unsafe to walk the streets. Under normal conditions Phnom Penh would be enjoying one of its beautiful, invigorating April days. But on this particular day, a thick layer of smoke blanketed the city, hiding the clear blue sky and bright sunshine.

Mother, my four sisters, and I (Vatha) were hustling around, cleaning up the breakfast dishes, making beds, planning the next meal, and generally straightening up the house. Father and my brothers were huddled close to the radio, where for hours they listened for more information from a station that had been on and off the air several times during the past few days.

Earlier that morning the regular programming of Buddhist prayers and traditional Cambodian music had given way to military marches. Then suddenly even the martial music stopped, and a man with a crusty voice announced the surrender of the Cambodian government to the Khmer Rouge. The official ceremonies took place on National Highway 5, just outside the city. The war was over. A new government was in the process of establishing itself.

Father was visibly relieved. In fact, he was emotional

when he said, "At last the massive killings will stop, for there will be no reason to continue."

Yes, this would be a tremendous relief for all of us. Estimates indicated that during the previous five years, as many as one half million men, women, and children had been killed or wounded, and thousands upon thousands more had been left homeless. Since neither side took prisoners, the fighting had been very brutal.

Another announcement sent shudders through the city. A Khmer Rouge spokesman boasted that the new government had not come to talk, but to act. Many officials of the former government should be hanged, he indicated. This proclamation caused leaders of the old government to flee to the Hotel Le Phnom, where the International Red Cross had set up headquarters.

A short time later Khmer Rouge soldiers, ignoring the large Red Cross flag flying in front of the Hotel, ordered the building emptied in 30 minutes, scattering those who had fled there for safety. About the same time, rumors spread in our neighborhood that all the inhabitants of the city were being forced out of their homes.

The report frightened me, but Father dismissed it as idle gossip. "Why," he reasoned, "would we be forced to leave our homes now? The change of government has already taken place."

※❀※

The 1960s

Back in the early 60s, few Cambodian politicians would have dreamed that the tiny Cambodian Communist Party might ever pose a threat to the nation. Actually, very few people even knew this group existed, for usually the party members hid out in the deep jungles or in the mountains. On one occasion, they staged a small rebellion in the Battambang area, but Prince Norodom Sihanouk, the leader of Cambodia, quickly quashed the revolt.

1970

Soon after Prime Minister Lon Nol had replaced Prince Sihanouk as leader of Cambodia, a shooting war erupted. After having been ousted from the government, the prince made a move that surprised many people—he joined the communist Khmer Rouge, the very party he had hunted for years, the organization he had been so determined to destroy. In an effort to win support for the overthrow of the Lon Nol government, the prince and the Khmer Rouge promised the poor farmers homes, cars, money, and the pleasures of city life if they would help.

Killings and terrorism on a small scale had been going on for a long time in Cambodia. Now it intensified when Prime Minister Lon Nol ousted Prince Sihanouk. Very soon it became more than just an occasional killing here and there, developing into a long civil war.

1971

Due to the overwhelming success of the Khmer Rouge in the countryside. Prime Minister Lon Nol dissolved the National Assembly and declared a state of emergency. During this year he suffered a stroke that left him paralyzed on his right side, causing him to spend considerable time in his office and making it difficult for him to get around.

1972

Early in the year the prime minister took another step to strengthen himself. He declared himself president of the Khmer Republic. About the same time, on the other side of the world, President Richard Nixon was reelected to a second term in a landslide victory.

1973

President Lon Nol ordered a general mobilization of all men up to 35 years of age. The Khmer Rouge had become a serious threat to the future of the nation. Fierce battles raged all around Phnom Penh, and it was difficult to get ample supplies into the city.

1974

Cambodia has only two seasons, the wet and the dry. During the heavy rains and floods of the rainy seasons, it was impossible for either side to carry on the war. But during the dry seasons of the past three years, the rockets of the Khmer Rouge had regularly exploded around our home. The new year had just been ushered in when it started again. The only difference this time was the intensified daily barrage of deadly fire from the sky. On one occasion, the artillery fire and rockets kept falling like rain for days.

Phnom Penh, the capital of the nation, was not the only place staggering under the terror of the Khmer Rouge. The whole country was suffering. According to a story circulating in the city and credited to the American ambassador, the Khmer Rouge had burned an entire village near Siem Reap, killing more than 60 people. In this attack they had not been content just to burn the village and kill the people. Before torching the buildings, they had nailed the elderly women to the walls of their homes and literally ripped the children apart.

Late in the year the rebels succeeded in blocking all major highways coming into Phnom Penh, cutting off the city's main source of food and leaving the Mekong River and the airport as the only supply routes. Immediately food became scarce and prices soared.

1975

With the arrival of the new year, refugees trying to escape the ruthless torture of the Khmer Rouge thronged Phnom Penh, causing the normal population of 600 thousand to explode to more than two million. The dry season brought the war back in all its fury. Up to now, the rainy season had enabled the city to build up its supplies, but the roadblocks now prevented that.

Usually the only individuals getting handouts on the streets of Phnom Penh were the saffron-robed (saffron is a yellow-orange dye and flavoring made from a purple crocus) Buddhist monks known as *bonzes*. But the picture had changed; now scores of men and women were begging. Also hundreds of homeless, starving children with distended bellies listlessly roamed the city in search of something to sustain life. Each evening they retreated to their cardboard shelters in the alleys or the outskirts of the city.

Rich people arranged to get their children out of the country. But Father did not have the money to get his family out. Even if money had been available, I don't think he would have sent us away. A number of different governments had come and gone during his time, and in each case he was able to get along. So he saw no reason why things would be different under the Khmer Rouge.

Early in the year, the Khmer Rouge succeeded in mining the Mekong River, blocking all river traffic. The regular three per week convoys of boats loaded with ammunition, fuel, rice, and other goods were stopped. The Khmer Rouge's bamboo floats, bobbing in the water of the Mekong, plainly reminded every ship captain that the river was mined. This action successfully cut the last free flow of supplies to the city. After the blockade, only one convoy managed to get through, and it was badly damaged. The severe shortages that followed caused gasoline rationing.

In an attempt to completely shut the door on the supplies of food and guns reaching the city, the Khmer Rouge showered the airport with hundreds of rockets—all in one day. Then day after day they continued hitting our last lifeline for supplies.

At this desperate time of need, the United States came to our rescue by beginning an airlift into Phnom Penh's Pochentong Airfield. It was a lifesaver for the city. Once it got under full operation, a cargo plane landed every few minutes, bringing in hundreds of tons of rice and munitions. It became an all-out effort to keep the Cambodian military operating and the people eating. This act of mercy kept our city from experiencing total famine, but it did not prevent slow starvation among thousands of children and poor people.

Continued rocket attacks forced us to make changes in our home. The three walls of the first floor were constructed of cement, but the second floor and a large part of the front of the house was of wood. My brothers corrected part of this problem by filling sacks with dirt and building a wall about three feet out in front of the house. When explosions rocked the city, everyone on the second floor would scramble down the narrow stairway and around the sharp right turn near the bottom to seek the protection of the concrete walls. If we were outside when the shelling erupted, we would jump into a bomb shelter at the side of the front yard.

One evening about 8:00, the house shook, rocked by an explosion that sounded as though it might be just next door. Screaming with fright, we dashed down the stairs, but nothing further happened. After we spent an uneasy night, daylight revealed that several nearby homes had been completely destroyed—houses that had been only 100 yards from our home. Lim and Father found fragments of the rocket on our roof.

As the Khmer Rouge continued tightening their grip on Phnom Penh, embassies worked round the clock to evacuate personnel. From the balcony of our home, our family watched the drama at the American Embassy. It started about 9:00 on the morning of April 12 as a wave of giant helicopters swept in over the city and unloaded United States soldiers near the embassy. Other helicopters—in groups of three—noisily followed. We could also see high overhead a large number of American fighter planes flying in circles, no doubt in position to protect the rescue operation.

The Khmer Rouge apparently respected the potential firepower of those high-flying jets and did not attempt to destroy the landing field. This restraint surprised us, because one of the Khmer Rouge gun emplacements was located very close to the U.S. Embassy. Almost two hours later, with the personnel evacuated, American Ambassador John Gunther Dean carried the United States flag along with the Cambodian flag of red, blue, and white to a waiting helicopter. Then in a storm of dust and the noise of rotor blades, he disappeared.

Throughout the nation, a small but brave Cambodian army continued to fight courageously against the Khmer

Rouge troops, which had increased in size to a reported 70,000. In Phnom Penh the army, from its dug-in positions and backed by our small outdated air force, defended the city.

Our military outlook was serious, because our troops were no match for the Khmer Rouge. In fact, the Cambodian fighting force was demoralized, poorly organized, and backed by a government steeped in corruption. Many of our soldiers had not received any pay for months. Throughout the country dishonest Cambodian army commanders regularly reported more soldiers under their command than were actually in their ranks and pocketed the pay of the missing soldiers when it arrived each month.

Month after month our troops continued to suffer heavy casualties. In a desperate move to recruit more men for the army, the government raised the age for draftees to 50. But it was too late even for these drastic measures. The war was about over. The vise-like grip of the Khmer Rouge on the city was strangling it.

President Lon Nol assembled a new cabinet and changed the army chief of staff, but these actions were too late and too little. The Khmer Rouge hit the ammunition depot at Phnom Penh's Pochentong Airport with a rocket, causing a warehouse of explosives to burst into an unquenchable sea of flames, littering the airport with debris, and disrupting the American airlift.

Soon the news reached us that our president had fled the country. Some maintained that he had deserted us, escaping to the safety of the exotic island of Bali. Others felt he had done this to make it easier to negotiate a peace settlement with the Khmer Rouge. Either way, it came as a serious blow and meant our situation was desperate.

Shortly after President Lon Nol's departure, the United States announced it was suspending our lifeline, the airlift. They blamed the continuing heavy attacks on the airport. This meant no more food—or guns. The supplies our army was depending on to check the advancing Khmer Rouge would be cut off. Food the city needed to survive would stop coming in, leaving more than two million people with a reported 10-day supply. Phnom Penh had become totally dependent on American support.

These two events acted as the proverbial straw that broke the camel's back. The city was doomed. All we could do was await our fate at the hands of the notoriously cruel Khmer Rouge.

On Thursday, April 17, 1975, their troops marched unopposed into the city.

❈

Thursday, April 17, 1975

The radio announcement that we had a new government roused Father's curiosity. Wanting to know what was going on, he and Mother set out to investigate. Walking down our narrow street to Mao Tse Tong Boulevard, they came face-to-face with the troops of the Khmer Rouge. The soldiers detained them a few moments then sent them home. Back home, Father ordered the family to get the packing completed immediately.

As the day wore on, our neighborhood was unusually quiet, dead—nothing moved. Even the dogs refused to bark, causing a deathly silence that was scary.

Early in the afternoon several *yotear* (the Khmer Rouge word for soldier or soldiers), wearing strange pajama-like black uniforms and a red-and-white checkered scarf around their necks, appeared on our street.

Late in the afternoon, I peeked through the curtains and spotted a yotear—just a boy in his early teens—heading for our house. His uniform was dirty and ragged, but he was carrying his rifle at the ready as he marched through our yard and pounded on the door. We could hear the yotear's high-pitched voice throughout the house as he shouted when Father opened our door, "Get out of the city. It will be bombed by the Americans. You can return home in a few days. But get out now. Hurry!" With that blunt announcement, he left.

American bombers had attacked Cambodia in the past. At one time, thousands of North Vietnamese troops were

18

gathered in the border area. During that time, American planes dropped hundreds of bombs on Cambodian territory in an attempt to break up the supply lines of the North Vietnamese. But we expected nothing of the sort from the Americans at this time. They were our friends. Until only a short time before this, they had supplied the city with food and guns.

After this abrupt order to abandon our home, events moved swiftly. We packed in earnest, each one trying to decide what to take. Mother put rice on the stove for the evening meal. All over the house questions ricocheted back and forth. Should I take this? That? Where should we go?

In the business section of the city it was the same. Khmer Rouge yotear moved from shop to shop and ordered the owners out at gunpoint. What Father originally thought was idle gossip was turning out to be true. The people of the entire city were being forced to flee into the countryside.

Across our street a group of yotear occupied the home of my cousin. She bargained with them as to the time she would have to leave the city, suggesting that since they were taking her home, they should give her the privilege of staying overnight at our home. They agreed, and we understood this permission that she had obtained to apply also to us.

It was near 6:00 in the early evening, and our rice was cooked. Some of us had already started eating when a motorcycle pulled up across the street. Obviously some kind of officer, the yotear had a handgun strapped to his side. But instead of going into my cousin's home, the officer strode across the street to our home, where candles were burning. His knock was hard and demanding and his voice stern as he ordered us out of the house immediately.

My cousin rushed to the door to explain the permission given her by the soldiers just a few hours before, but the officer paid no attention. His eyes narrowed, and pointing his pistol at her, he said, "See this. Get out now, right now, or I'll kill you." Panic set in. Some of the family dashed out as the officer walked away. A few picked up bundles as they made their exit.

As we walked down the street, we could easily see that our neighbors had already left. Father was convinced we would be able to return soon, so we stopped in front of a neighbor's house. But it was only a few moments before a yotear ordered us on. During the short mile before we reached the main boulevard, we stopped several times, but a yotear cut short each stop.

The sight at Monivong Boulevard was unexpected. I could hardly believe my eyes. The beautiful, wide boulevard was swarming with frightened, bewildered people—all heading in one direction. Our once proud Phnom Penh, with its tree-lined boulevards, its French-style cafes, its beautiful mansions and villas surrounded with tropical foliage, was in total confusion and would soon be empty. The people were pouring into the streets as they fled the guns of the Khmer Rouge.

In the almost solid pack of humanity, cars were being pushed for lack of gasoline. Only a few were creeping along at a snail's pace. Scattered here and there were motorcycles, pedicabs, bicycles piled high with household items, and bullock carts jammed with people and their precious possessions. Surrounding all the vehicles and carts were throngs of old people, young people, mothers carrying their young children on their hips, and men loaded with sewing machines, televisions, and other valuables.

Earlier in the day, at one of Phnom Penh's hospitals, the Khmer Rouge had forced a French surgeon to stop operating on a wounded patient. Hospitals were emptied, and some of the sick—still lying in their hospital beds—were being pushed along the boulevard. Shutters and windows were broken in empty homes, and soldiers were looting shops and robbing people on the street. Confusion was everywhere.

The moment we edged into this congested mass, it pushed us toward the river. Soldiers, trying to get the people moving faster, were firing their guns into the air, but the flood of humanity just kept inching along. In a few blocks we worked our way out of the mass of people. Father, still convinced we would be able to return home soon, suggested that we not go too far away, but yotear ordered us on, cutting short our stop.

Another mile and we arrived at the school known as the Faculty of Law (Law School), with its beautiful grounds. The large expanse of green grass and graceful palms gave it a sense of calm, a good place to stop for the night.

Stretching out on the grass and looking up that evening of Thursday, April 17, I could see the stars shining through the palm leaves. A pleasant breeze was blowing, and I could hear only faintly the noise on the street. But the past 12 hours had been a dreadful nightmare, impossible for me to comprehend. My thoughts were confused as they bounced back and forth between the past and present.

Mother busied herself in making everyone as comfortable as possible. While watching her, I realized how good my parents were and what a peaceful home I had enjoyed. But now we were running from an army that had just taken over our city. The prospects of the future gripped me with fear, a kind of fear I had never known before.

Memories of the past flooded my mind. With them came my first real memory of Father. We had been living in Laos, where he served as the second highest official in the Cambodian Embassy, sent there soon after he had returned from the United Nations.

A friend at the embassy had given him the recipe for making ice cream in a refrigerator. After a wait, which seemed to me more like days than hours, the ice cream had properly frozen and Father dished it out with considerable ceremony. In a teasing manner my older brother, Leng, tried to grab my ice cream, but Father cut short his fun, using a fan to administer a gentle swat. Dad's gesture shocked Leng so much that he lost control, wetting his pants.

The memory of Father's trip to the United Nations in November of 1958 was also vivid. Having been told about it so many times, I remembered it clearly, even though I had been just a baby when it took place. Prince Sihanouk headed the Cambodian delegation, which included the Cambodian Royal Dancers. When he arrived in New York City, Father was sick, causing him to cut short his original intentions of staying a number of months.

Later events indicated he had visited the United States long enough to notice American cars, for soon after returning home he bought a new Buick. It was among the first of its kind in the country as most of our cars came from France or Japan.

Father was well educated for a Cambodian. Before going into government work and getting married at age 22, he had graduated from high school and had taken work at the law school.

After having served for two years in Laos, Father was appointed assistant administrator of Stung Treng province. Officials who served the Cambodian government received a good salary. I remember Father receiving $800 a month in American money at a time when the average Cambodian family received the equivalent of $100 American dollars a year. Because so many Cambodians lived in poverty, Father strongly opposed his family spending money on the jewelry and expensive clothes that we girls, of course, coveted. He felt it was dangerous to show wealth.

Father believed in democracy, running his household in a participatory manner. One of his assignments had paid him a large amount of money. Before spending it, he assembled the family to decide how we should use it. The practical ones wanted to add another bathroom to our home. Certainly it was needed with a family of 12 evenly divided between male and female. But the adventurous, fun-loving section of the family favored taking a trip to Angkor Wat, one of the famous old temples. We took the trip.

Father read many books that included medical as well as political subjects. As I lay on the grass and gazed up through the palm trees to the stars, I could visualize him studying his French medical book. As a result of the knowledge he gained from this book, it had never been necessary for me to visit a doctor. When one of us became sick, Father would note the symptoms, consult his book, and buy the necessary medicine. Much of his reading in the political field came from France and Russia and concerned communism. The theory of a classless society fascinated him. The thought of no more poverty was especially appealing, but he never supported these theories or joined movements based on them.

I also remembered my one and only whipping. Father always liked to take a short rest after lunch. As a rule Mother had only one job during his nap time, keeping us quiet. One afternoon she had forgotten all about keeping us tranquil, and we children also had a complete lapse of memory. But our forgetfulness was short-lived, for soon Father stood in the door, his usual smile missing. In calm but stern language, he ordered us into the living room. As we were following his orders he went out into the yard, returning in a few moments with a stick. Father was a man of few words. None were really needed at this time for we knew exactly the mistake we had made, and it was not hard to guess the punishment due us. Standing at one end of the room, he called us over one by one, turned us around, and administered a sound whipping.

My memory drifted back to the extra work Father did in addition to his government duties, tasks such as writing a daily column for each of the two newspapers in Phnom Penh—the French, *La Press*, and the Cambodian, *Meatophoum*. Also, he had written and published two books of fiction—a story of his country and a love story.

Trouble began the day one of his poems alluding to the corruption and waste in the national government was published. The next day he found plainclothesmen following him and spying on our home. Although he was never a communist, it would have been hard to prove after the publication of his poem, especially if someone had found communist books in his library. Realizing a search might come at any time, we hurriedly burned the books. Nothing serious came of the incident, but I vividly remembered the consternation it brought us.

It would be hard to forget our home of 18 years, the one we had just left behind. In spite of Father's work, which required him to serve in different parts of the country and sometimes out of the country, he never gave up our home in

Phnom Penh. It was a nice two-story brick structure covered with white plaster and crowned with a tile roof. The 11 rooms provided plenty of space for our large family. My cousin, who lived across the street, had arranged for her home to be hooked up to city lights and water. Father had purchased an electric meter and a water meter so we could buy these services from her. We, in turn, sold lights and water to the neighbors on either side of us. These conveniences had added to our enjoyment. This house was the only real home I knew, because we had moved in a month after I had been born.

Then there were the memories of Mother, a good house-keeper and treasurer for the family. Mother's handling the money was not unusual in Cambodia, for women were highly respected members of the family.

Mother didn't sing very often, but I can still hear her soft voice as she would quietly sing the old traditional lullaby, cuddling me in her arms and gently caressing my hair. She pressed her nose against my cheek as she inhaled, giving me a Cambodian kiss. Our family revolved around Mother, who held it together with her love and kindness.

Phnom Penh was a beautiful city, my birthplace, capital of the nation. I loved its wide, shady boulevards, beautiful parks, and charming squares. Life in the city moved at a slower pace than in most Western cities. In this land of soft and gentle living, we were not rushed, but there was sufficient activity to make life interesting. Most of the conveniences of the West could be secured for a little money. Food was plentiful in the covered market of Phnom Penh and the French-style cafes. It was a pleasure to live in Phnom Penh.

The countryside, where most of the people lived, was beautiful with its thick tropical jungles, palm trees, great rivers, forested mountains, and rice paddies. Food was abundant for most of the people. Almost anyone could get rice. In many places fish were just waiting for a bait, trap, or net.

I was 18—a recent graduate from high school and looking forward to additional education. Little did I realize how much my life would change as a result of the events of the past few hours. For 55 months I would be a slave, homeless and hungry. I didn't know it then, but a long dark night was just beginning.

Friday, April 18, 1975

The sun glistened on the wet palm leaves when I awoke the next morning. My clothes were damp from the morning dew, and my back ached from having slept on the ground. The surrounding beauty contrasted starkly to my feelings. What seemed like a horrible nightmare the night before was, indeed, a living reality. Even as I awakened, the noise from the street drove home the plight of our family. Like us, thousands were fleeing the guns of the Khmer Rouge.

After a quick meal of rice, we melted into the crush of frightened people heading for the river. There we learned that some residents of Phnom Penh, overwhelmed by the thought of living under the Khmer Rouge, had driven their cars into the water, killing themselves and their families.

Father was still entertaining a strong conviction of returning home soon. Consequently, we stopped when he found a house we could camp under. A quick check of our supplies brought devastating news. Most of the essential items, such as rice and plastic, we'd left back home. Mother had a little money, however, so she bought a 12-inch pan for 4,000 *riels* (Cambodian dollars). Another 500 riels bought one eggplant. This was the last time she used Cambodian money, for it soon became useless, disappearing along with the banks and postal service.

April and May 1975

While camping near the river, a cousin of mine who was fleeing with us suddenly remembered a school paper he had prepared about the Khmer Rouge. Trying to be honest with his statements, he had said things that were not complimentary about them. Like Father, he expected we would soon be able to return home. The thought of the new rulers finding this paper made him very uneasy. It bothered him so much that he talked to Father about the possibility of returning to the city and destroying the paper. Certain that the Khmer Rouge would kill him without hesitation, Father was afraid of this plan and did his best to change my cousin's mind, but the next day he along with another cousin turned up missing. Knowing Father was opposed to their returning to the city, they had slipped away for Phnom Penh without bidding us goodbye. We learned later that the Khmer Rouge were in fact killing people who tried to return to the city. No one has seen or heard of those two cousins since.

Getting water required stepping over bloated, decomposing bodies near the river. Every two or three days we moved a short distance, always foraging for food. Styles, names, and customs began changing. All the Khmer Rouge girls wore short hair. Later we learned the Khmer Rouge wanted everyone, men and women, to look alike. Long hair for women was apparently too feminine for their tastes and ideology.

Khmer Rouge yotear kept asking us girls a perplexing question. Were we a *neary* or a *satrei*? We did not understand them at first. It sounded like they were asking whether we were girls or women. Finally we learned they were trying to determine whether we were married or single.

While we waited for permission to return home, a special National Congress convened in Phnom Penh. Its purpose was organizing the new government, outlining the policy of death to those opposing it, and changing the name of the country. No longer did we live in Cambodia, but Democratic Kampuchea.

Also the Khmer Rouge were busy sealing off the country so the outside world would not hear of the terrible suffering caused by the forced exodus of the general population. Nor would they learn of the goal of the Khmer Rouge to cause the population to forget all "degenerate" foreign influences and to purge them of all Western thoughts and desires. The horrible cruelty of the Khmer Rouge was to be sealed in. Under their plans, there would be no leaking of information to the outside world.

To accomplish this blackout all airports were closed, all roads blocked, and all communication with the outside world was cut off. Land was cleared of all inhabitants along the Kampuchea-Thai border, and mines were planted to discourage Kampucheans from fleeing and others from entering the country. The record shows that they succeeded in keeping the world in ignorance about Kampuchea. We were sealed into a life of unimaginable misery and death.

Soon we learned that the slaughtering of those who opposed the new government had commenced. The radio indicated that some of the leaders of Lon Nol's government had already been beheaded. Also the Khmer Rouge were rounding up the defeated soldiers and killing them.

A brutal bloodbath was reported nearby. According to the stories, trucks filled with former Lon Nol soldiers were being driven into the area. As the Khmer Rouge soldiers unloaded the Lon Nol soldiers, they clubbed them to death. After the killings, local village men were required to dig graves for the dead soldiers, then the villagers were told to plow the field where the graves were located. When they objected, the village official insisted that they comply. The startled villagers were told the corpses would make good fertilizer for the crops.

In a nearby village another upsetting event took place. A Cambodian lady who had worked as a receptionist for the British Embassy returned home to her village after having been forced out of Phnom Penh. In her work she occasionally took guests of the embassy to a restaurant for dinner.

Back in the village she was accused of being an international prostitute and was arrested. Her sister maintained she was a good woman, trying to explain that being a receptionist and taking people out to dinner was respectable work. After a few days the leader called a meeting of all the villagers. The 22-year-old receptionist was marched under guard to the gathering place. The leader explained the charge. He pronounced this lady an evil woman—an international prostitute for the British Embassy—and as such deserving of death. He went on to say that this woman was so evil that she didn't deserve just to die. She must serve as an example so others would not be tempted to follow her immoral ways.

The suggestion he then made caused most of the villagers to catch their breath in disbelief. Her clothing must be stripped from her and her breasts cut from her body before she was executed. Among those gathered for the event was the accused's sister, who knew it would be sure death for her if she made any effort to defend her sister. Men soon arrived with huge knives. As the butchers started the brutal task of cutting off the young lady's breasts, her sister could stand it no longer. With her emotions out of control she screamed, "No! No!" and fell to the ground.

After the bloody murder of the receptionist was completed, the village leader told his men to bring the sister forward, the one who had cried out. Without any show of feelings, he calmly explained to the speechless people that this woman was also very wicked because she had cried out for her sister and was shedding tears for her. Therefore, she also deserved death. The shocked villagers witnessed another execution.

It was fortunate that Father took us along the river after leaving Phnom Penh. In this area the yotear did not push us, demanding we walk faster. Some travelers going in other directions were forced to maintain a brutal pace in their march or risk being killed. Many of the sick, old, and children were left behind to die because they could not keep walking fast enough to please the yotear.

Each day our pursuit of food became more intense. A month had slipped by, and we still had no prospects of returning home. This, plus our critically low food supply, forced Father to reluctantly give up all hope of seeing home again. My oldest sister, Sour Ly, had a mother-in-law living about 31 miles from Phnom Penh in the direction we were going. If she was still alive and in her own home, she could help us.

That evening Father made arrangements for us to ride on a boat, but before boarding the next morning, I saw a sight that both surprised and frightened me. Arriving on the boats, which were turning around at this river port, were a large number of "old people." This designation was given to the people who had been under the control of the Khmer Rouge for several years.

I was startled. They were so thin, actually more like walking skeletons. Smiles never creased their faces, and they moved like robots—slow and deliberate. Their clothes were ragged and patched so many times that I couldn't determine the original fabric.

As our family moved slowly through their camp, we were speechless. While waiting to board the boat, we said very little. Slowly the jolt of seeing all those starving people came into focus. Was it possible we were looking at ourselves a year from now? Would this be our fate too? But we had no time to ponder these questions, the boat was leaving soon. Urged by the yotear, we hurried on board expecting a long ride, but without explanation we were ordered off at the next stop.

An hour later, as we trudged past a small village, an armed man in a black pajama uniform ordered us to show our travel papers. We had none. In fact, the idea of getting permission to travel was entirely new to us. It was one of the new ways the Khmer Rouge used to control the people. Without official permission to travel, we were forced to follow him to the village. (See the map on next page.)

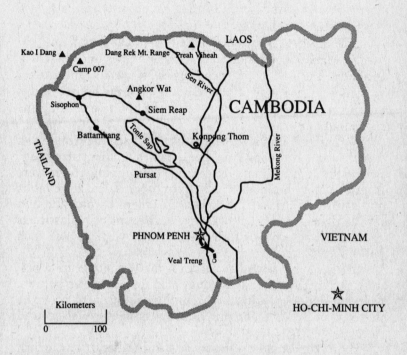

Kao I Dang ▲

Camp 007 ▲

Dang Rek Mt. Range

Preah Viheah ▲

LAOS

Sen River

CAMBODIA

Angkor Wat ▲

Sisophon

Siem Reap ●

Tonle Sap

Battambang

Konpong Thom ◎

Mekong River

Pursat

THAILAND

PHNOM PENH ☆

Veal Treng

VIETNAM

HO-CHI-MINH CITY ☆

Kilometers

0   100

May 1975

Within a few minutes the village leader found a place for us to live, one of the better wooden homes already occupied by two other families. Our arrival increased the number of occupants to 22. Before leaving, the leader ordered us to report for work the next morning and to attend the village meeting that evening.

Only a short distance from the river, Veal Treng, our new village, consisted of about 50 wooden homes and thatched-roof huts. Located in a farming region, it was like most other villages—no stores or public buildings. All the houses in this area were on stilts to keep them above the river during the monsoons.

We had to climb a 10-foot ladder to reach the front door. The one big room had no beds, tables, chairs, or closets. Below the living room, the kitchen and dining room were finished off with a packed dirt floor, open sides, large table, and a stove of bricks and stones. Our utensils consisted of a few tin plates, spoons, a fork or two, chopsticks, a plastic gas container that was used for water, a few bowls, and a 12-inch pan for cooking.

Clothes were stored in *sarongs*, the Kampuchean ladies' long skirts. These handy sarongs also served as our pillows. Mats on the floor, with the needful mosquito nets, took the place of beds. At night our house was nearly wall-to-wall sleepers.

The path behind the house led to the bathroom, which was nothing more than a hole in the ground, with two strong boards over it to stand on. Water and dry banana leaves served as toilet tissue. The shower, with its walls of banana leaves and a pitcher holding about two quarts of water, was in the same area.

Each day the village leader provided a half can of uncooked rice for each person. The container used for measuring was about the size of a small Campbell's soup can. To stretch our food, Mother prepared our rice with a generous amount of water, which helped fill our empty stomachs, making the meal more satisfying at the time.

Once established in our new home, Father set out to find my sister's mother-in-law. Only a few days passed before he returned with her, and both were carrying as much food as possible on their bicycles. What a treat for a hungry family— extra rice, potatoes, sugar, corn, and bananas!

Sour Ly's mother-in-law had secured a letter giving her permission to leave her village for two nights. As her time to return home grew near, almost everyone wanted to accompany her, for she had plenty of food growing on her land. But too large a group could present a problem. She could take my sister and her son because they were her close relatives. The village leader would likely reject all others. Father eventually persuaded her to take two more, my sister Letine and my brother Saat.

Every morning I reported to a feisty taskmaster for my work assignment. She was a belligerent young Kampuchean from the country and was known as one of the "old people." We were the "new people," the slaves of the "old people." I can still see her, hands on hips, standing on a tree stump, and shouting orders.

Work usually consisted of weeding rice paddies, cutting grass for thatched roofs, digging irrigation ditches, and clearing land. Supplied with a shovel, I was required to dig a ditch 15 feet long, 2 feet wide, and 2 feet deep. The loose dirt was used to build a bank on the sides, and I had to complete the job in a single day. Equipment was always scarce. In some villages the "new people" were digging ditches with sticks or even with their bare hands. Others, in villages without oxen, were hitched to plows.

When we were assigned to weed a rice paddy, it became a disaster. Being city girls, neither my sister By nor I had ever set foot in a rice paddy. At the end of our first long day of backbreaking work, our leader checked what we had done and found that we had uprooted all the rice plants, leaving only the weeds. She was indignant and promptly spread the news about the pinheaded city girls who knew nothing about farming.

On another day snickering broke out as we returned from

cutting grass for thatching roofs. The leader was irate, and the other girls made fun of us. Our bundles of grass were small compared to theirs, and we were carrying them on our hips not on our heads, where, according to them, such burdens belonged. The leader decided to teach us a lesson. She and the farm girls gathered more grass, then tied it in with my bundle, making it very heavy. Requiring me to kneel down, she placed the heavy bundle on my head. Then she stood back, with hands on her hips, and told me to stand up and walk. I tried—tried real hard—but couldn't get up. Raising her voice, she again ordered me to stand up. I strained every muscle but failed once more. Her anger mounted and she screamed at me, accusing me of pretending, threatening me, but I couldn't get up even if my life had depended on it. The bundle was too heavy. After laughing at me and calling me all kinds of names, she and the girls walked away in disgust. They left me on the ground with the heavy bundle still on my head.

Even if we did not know the difference between weeds and rice plants and were unable to carry heavy loads of grass on our heads, we did have one advantage over the others. We had studied both French and English in school, so when we wanted to talk without others understanding, these languages came in handy. While the farm girls resented our ability to communicate in this way, it was fun and provided us the occasion to laugh at them—secretly, of course.

We did not realize it then, but speaking in English or French could have resulted in our death because it was evidence that we were educated. Fortunately, neither the work leader nor the farm girls caught on to this slip.

In the meeting that came soon after work, the village leader reminded everyone of how thankful he or she should be for the Khmer Rouge. He called them our liberators, those who saved us from the corruption of the former government. Following his long speech, he announced that after singing we would have a session of *kosang*.

This time the singing meant the national anthem of Democratic Kampuchea, which was sung at almost every meeting. True to the revolutionary nature of the anthem, it talked a great deal about blood covering the towns and plains. I stood with the rest to sing, moving my lips, but not joining in the murderous words.

When we had finished singing, the village leader moved right into kosang, which is an opportunity for anyone to accuse another of wrongdoing. I held my breath. Both *By* and I were guilty of pulling up the rice plants instead of the weeds. But no one said anything about our mistakes. Others were criticized, however, then the criticized person had to stand up, acknowledge the mistake, repent, and promise to correct the fault.

The Khmer Rouge leaders had another tool that was really frightening. Many of them required all the villagers to write out a biography of their life. This history was to be complete, including where they were born, name of their parents, school attended, amount of education, and previous occupation. What if our village leader required a biography? Father was well educated and a former government official. *By* and I were high school graduates. It could mean death for all of us.

The Khmer Rouge were looking for anyone associated with the former government—army officers, soldiers, civil servants, teachers, and policemen. Also they were suspicious of merchants, doctors, monks, and anyone who showed a talent in leadership. When detected, these people were usually executed.

Phnom Penh was a major holdout against the Khmer Rouge and contained an unusually high percentage of people who fiercely opposed them. Knowing this, the Khmer Rouge were looking for these people. As a result many of the former residents of the city changed their names or used only their first name.

July 1975

Desperate for extra food, Father sent Lim across the river to Sour Ly's mother-in-law's place to get additional supplies. Letine decided to ride back with him to help carry extra food plus to deliver a special message to Mother. She had just about reached home when she came to several guards patrolling the road. They demanded her travel papers. She had some that allowed her to go only as far as the river. Now she was well passed the river. The guards held her a short time, fined her a large bag of rice, and released her.

As she continued on, the front wheel of her bike slid in the mud, and she fell off. Lim was ahead and did not see the accident, but when Letine failed to show up, he hurried back and found her just regaining consciousness.

Despite the blow to her head, Letine did not forget her special message for Mother. It concerned Sour Ly's baby, which was due to be born very soon. Naturally, Mother wanted to be present at this important time, so she left early the next morning with Letine.

They had not gone far when Father received orders to move his family to Battambang, 155 miles away. The continual scarcity of food caused the government to arrange for a general migration westward, taking the people to the rice rather than the rice to the people. Quickly Father dispatched Lim to bring Mother and the others back to our village. But before this was possible, early the next day, Father was directed to take his family to the village center. He waited a short time, but finally, without the rest of the family, we had to start out. We had no choice, stalling would cause suspicion.

Living under the iron hand of the Khmer Rouge, we learned to listen carefully and act promptly when officials spoke. When they said move, it was necessary to move quickly, without argument and without questions or complaints. Had Father attempted to explain our problem, he would have been in trouble, likely accused of complaining. Also it would have revealed that Mother had traveled out of the village without permission from the leader. Father was wise in not saying anything to the leader about a delay.

It was dark when we reached the river, which was large, something like the Mississippi. Small canoe-like boats without lights were ferrying people to the other side, where the big boat would anchor. The ride across in the dark was terribly frightening, and no life belts were provided. On the other side, things were not going right. The men were having trouble getting near the bank, and Father was trying to help by calling out instructions.

Once Father was on the bank, a lady stepped up to him—Mother. When she had heard that we were moving, she came directly to the river port and had recognized Father's voice when he shouted instructions to the boatmen. Our family was back together again, but our joy faded as we learned the news Mother had brought. Sour Ly wanted to travel west with us, but the baby was due, making it almost impossible for Sour Ly to travel. Under these circumstances, Sour Ly decided it best to stay with her mother-in-law.

A quick check of our surroundings the next morning showed people swarming all over the riverbank. The air was foul because there were no toilet facilities. Rain, driven by the wind, buffeted us. Firewood was scarce and wet. But rice had to be cooked before boarding time, so Mother and Saat rushed off in search of wood.

Since hundreds of people had been looking for this important fuel, they were forced to walk about half a mile before finding a few small sticks. As Saat was filling his basket, a yotear surprised him, charging him with running away from his work project. He then tied Saat to a tree. Mother explained our need and that we were traveling on the boat, but it made no difference. The yotear refused to release Saat. Noon came, and my brother was still tied up.

Just before dark he was released. Picking up the needed wood, Mother and Saat made their way back to the loading area in the darkness. The rice was cooked, and we boarded the boat just before it pulled away from the dock. Once again our family was fortunate. Any contact with the yotear was always risky. These men were trigger-happy and reckless with their authority. All this caused us to live in constant fear.

Late the next day as we approached the river junction known as Four Arms, we caught sight of Phnom Penh. Here the Mekong River splits into two rivers flowing south. From the northwest the Tonle Sap joins it. The Tonle Sap is especially interesting since it is both a river and a lake and flows in two different directions, depending on the season of the year.

The lake part of the Tonle Sap is a third larger than the Great Salt Lake in Utah and acts as an overflow basin for the floodwater of the mighty Mekong. It expands from a width of two miles in the dry season to more than six miles during the monsoons.

Fishing on the Tonle Sap is among the best in the world. As the monsoon-swollen Mekong sends its extra water into the Tonle Sap lake, trees in the lowlands surrounding the lake are flooded up to their lower branches. Fish coming from the Mekong lay their eggs in the branches of these trees. When the little fish hatch, they feed on the leaves and grow very rapidly. As the heavy rains cease, the Mekong begins to draw water from the Tonle Sap lake. The current soon becomes very swift, so much so that the water turns into a rushing torrent where the lake empties into the river. Fishing nets at this point can harvest huge quantities of fish.

Approaching Phnom Penh was a very emotional time for the family. Our home of 18 years was in this city, just a short distance from us, but we could not get off the boat. Moving slowly along, with no sound except the dull grinding of the engines to disturb the silence, each of us was isolated in his or her own thoughts.

I could see the Royal Palace—with its curving roofs rising above the high wall encircling it—the pinnacles of the Royal Pagoda, and the Audience Hall. Next we passed the Music Pavilion, where the Cambodian Royal Dancers practiced and performed their dance routines. It is a beautiful building, open on all sides, with white pillars holding up the roof. The pavilion was deserted, but in my imagination I could see it full of beautifully dressed young ladies performing their graceful dances.

In the early history of Cambodia, the dancers performed nude above the waist, were sewn into their fancy costumes, and were part of the king's harem. Additional girls were added to the king's harem from time to time in response to his desire or at the request of parents who were eager to give their daughters to the king. If the girl was accepted, the parents usually received a little money and maybe a few clothes. When these parents left the palace, there was little chance they would see their daughter again, but they had the satisfaction of knowing she was with the king.

Once a year the Water Festival took place on the river, just where we were passing. It consisted mainly of boats carved from the single trunk of a large tree and manned by a large crew of rowers. The competition took place before the king, his queen, and the royal household, who were either on the bank or in the royal junk along the shore. The king was always shaded by a beautiful parasol and attended by gorgeous palace ladies who waved fans of peacock feathers. Lining the banks of the river and in hundreds of boats were thousands upon thousands of people cheering for their favorite contestants.

In this same area Prince Sihanouk used to bless the waters of the river. His blessing did not come at any old time during the year but on the very day the waters of the Tonle Sap changed direction. As a result, many Cambodians thought that the prince had power to change the direction the river was flowing.

From the boat it was also possible to see Wat Phnom, the ancient temple on the hill from which our city took its name. One Cambodian tradition tells the story about a lady by the name of Penh who lived on the hill where the temple now stands. It seems that during the monsoon season a large koki tree trunk was deposited on the hill near her home. When the waters receded and she looked into the hollow space in the log, much to her surprise she found four bronze statues of Buddhas. Feeling the gods had blessed her in a special manner, she built a temple there, which became known as Wat Phnom or the temple on the hill. During the years that followed, a city grew up near the Hill Temple. The name of the city, legend indicates, comes from the Cambodian word *Phnom*, meaning hill, and the lady's name, *Penh*.

For a few minutes I forgot our plight, but as the boat

moved on, I was suddenly jerked back to reality. Today the area was quiet, no races on the water, no dancers performing in the Music Pavilion, and no king sitting on the bank. It was easy to see that Phnom Penh was in ruins, a ghost city cluttered with abandoned cars and empty shops.

Yet here was my home, so close yet so far away. Here were the streets and boulevards I knew so well, the hospital where I had been born, the government buildings where Father had worked, the public school I had attended, the big covered market where we had shopped, the beautiful park we used to visit. But all were beyond my reach and slowly drifting farther and farther away until they faded from sight. Tears trickled down my cheeks as we passed the old brick-yards outside the city. Sensing our sadness, Father tried to be optimistic by maintaining that we were heading in the right direction. He was right. The government was sending us toward the Thai border, which could mean freedom.

That night I tossed and turned. The emotional upset of being so close to home, yet barred from it, robbed me of sleep. As I stretched out on the deck and listened to the steady groan of the engines, I couldn't help wondering if all my dreams, my happiness, my freedom would be out of reach— just like our home.

A new day brought us to Kampong Chhnang, where my four hungry brothers lost no time in gathering wood for cooking. After a couple of days, army trucks arrived. We boarded them and endured a jolting ride to Pursat. Here the authorities instructed us to wait for a train.

During the delay we heard a horrifying story about mass killings. It was hard to determine in which section of the country the killings were taking place, but from the fragments of information coming from different individuals, we got the picture of a large number of people being affected. First, it seems, the women and children were taken in small groups into the woods, stripped of their clothes, blindfolded, and forced to march to the edge of deep hole in the ground, where they were compelled to kneel. Yotear would then strike them on the back of the neck with a club, and their bodies would tumble into the pit.

Next the men were put through the same process. The disturbing aspect was that we could not prove or disprove these rumors. Yet since we kept hearing similar stories time after time and saw our own evidence of the cruelty of the Khmer Rouge, we had no trouble believing what we heard, and we wondered when our time would come to kneel at the edge of a pit.

The freight train finally arrived. The boxcars we boarded had hauled cattle, but despite the filth and smell, it was still better than walking. The ride was short, yet the vegetation of the area changed dramatically. Only a few trees remained, and on every side we saw large rice fields. When we got off the train, we found another surprise. The officials were forming a new farm community about six miles from the road, and they ordered us to move there. This turn of events alarmed Father.

Mother and Letine were directed to arrange for our farm land. The news they brought back was both good and bad. A young man had approached Letine, recognizing her as the sister of a girl he had known at school. He was an old boyfriend of my sister *By*. That was the good news; we had found a friend. The bad news concerned the land they wanted us to start farming. It was very poor, had not been cultivated in the past, and was dry. Worst of all, no water was nearby, and the land was located off the main road. In fact, it was everything Father was determined to avoid.

Mother's report did not surprise Father. In his work he had traveled to this area and knew it well. But I was scared when he announced we would not go out into that worthless part of the country to farm, but would continue moving on toward the border. How could he make this possible?

The young man who had introduced himself to Letine came to Father with the request that he be permitted to join our family. For some time he had been separated from his mother, and his father was dead. Father accepted him.

While it was still dark the next morning, our little band of 10 was walking again, traveling west toward freedom. However, none of us had any official traveling permits. Fortunately Father had a plan. Several times he had seen official travel papers. So at a convenient stopping place, he produced some paper from his precious little supply. I was chosen as scribe. From his keen memory, Father dictated a letter using the special words found in the official authorization papers. The document was complete with two fake signatures—one by *By* and the other by Father.

Armed with this official-looking document granting us permission to visit Father's relatives in Battambang, we marched on feeling secure. The next village, Mong Russei, was noted for its rice production. Rice not only grew in the area surrounding Mong Russei, but the village was also known for its processing of rice. While most of the people in the country husked their rice with crude homemade tools, in this village rice was husked with big machinery. But when we arrived, the machinery was silent, most of it had been smashed by the Khmer Rouge.

Our excitement really exploded upon learning that trains were running between Mong Russei and Battambang every day, and Battambang was just 32 miles away. For the final part of our journey, we secured deluxe seats again—the floor of a boxcar.

As we scrambled off the train at the central railroad station in Battambang, we could see workers making preparations to move the train on to Sisophon, near the Thai border, our real goal. This electrifying turn of events caused our excited family to climb quickly back into the boxcar, but in a few minutes the yotear found us and demanded our travel papers.

The forged document didn't seem such a good idea with yotear surrounding us. Suddenly I realized we had overlooked one very important item. Our letter gave us permission to travel to Battambang, an evacuated city. No Khmer Rouge official in his right mind would be so foolish as to give such permission. Also, how was Father going to explain that we were still on the train, heading for the border, when our letter gave permission for travel only to Battambang? How was he going to talk his way out of this blunder?

My anxiety increased as a company of yotear surrounded Father, marching him off to see their officer. The official looked at the letter for a long time, while Father's heart pounded. He was sure the officer knew it was forged. All kinds of fearful eventualities rushed through his mind. There was a long pause, and when the officer finally spoke, he caught Father completely off guard. Without saying a word about the letter, the officer prohibited him from boarding the train again. Father felt so relieved, so surprised, that he lost his normal composure and tripped over his own sandal while bowing and trying to make a graceful exit.

A short train ride brought us to the area where my aunt was represented as living. But we could find no aunt. Others said they knew where she lived. Now we were walking again and facing an angry storm. Before reaching shelter, the sky opened up, drenching us, and causing us to spend half the night by the fire trying to dry our clothes. After a few hours of sleep, we were walking once again. Several rains later we found my Father's sister and, much to my surprise, my sister Nakry.

All agreed it would be wonderful if we could stay in their village, but we were living in Kampuchea, not free Cambodia. Freedom to live in the place of one's choice was denied. The big question was Will the Khmer Rouge leader allow us to stay in his village? My aunt went to see.

When she returned, we could see the answer written on her face. The village leader gave an emphatic no—her relatives would have to leave. However, she also had some good news. Her daughter was living in another village not too far away. As a leader of the women, she might be able to help. Her village was still in the Battambang area, and they accepted us.

Thanks to Father, we had made the trip to Battambang without becoming separated. He also had avoided taking his family to farm in a worthless part of the country and had managed to position his family some 62 miles from the Thai border. I was tired, but glad to know we were accepted and so close to freedom. Now it was possible to settle down for a short time while making plans for the next move. (See the map on next page.)

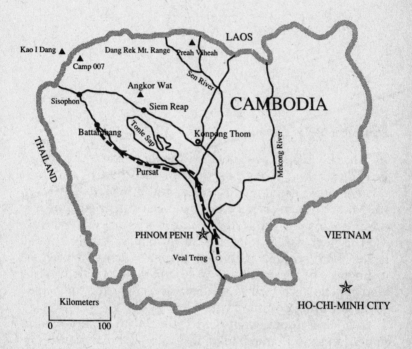

Kao I Dang ▲

Camp 007 ▲

Dang Rek Mt. Range

Preah Viheah ▲

LAOS

Sen River

CAMBODIA

Angkor Wat ▲

Sisophon

Siem Reap

Battambang

Tonle Sap

Konpong Thom

Pursat

THAILAND

Mekong River

PHNOM PENH ☆

VIETNAM

Veal Treng

Kilometers

0   100

HO-CHI-MINH CITY ☆

September 1975

Our new region was officially known as zone 4, sector 43. Under Lon Nol's government, the country had been divided into villages, towns, cities, and provinces. However, the Khmer Rouge changed this arrangement, organizing it in a way to give the top leaders control over every individual.

The next day Mother started husking rice with the old ladies. This prompt action on her part demonstrated the willingness of the family to work for their rice. It was the kind of action every village leader was looking for and helped get us off to a good start with him.

Land was soon assigned to Father, who took down an empty house in Battambang and hauled the material to our village. All nails, doors, tin, and other items were carefully preserved, for it was not possible to go to the local lumber yard to buy them, since there were no lumber yards or stores of any kind.

Father's finished product was long and narrow, about 10 feet by 22 feet, with a dirt floor and a lean-to at the side serving as the kitchen. Westerners entering our little home through the kitchen would have been impressed with our bed, which ran the full length of the building. It was made of wood, bench-like, and raised off the floor about 20 inches. Not only did it serve as our bed at night, but it also became our living and dining room during the day. The roof was the best we could get, grass. A door at each end of the house, plus one opening into the kitchen, and several "air conditioning windows"—with no glass—completed the design.

Around our new home rice paddies stretched out in every direction. It was a sparsely settled area. Except for one house and a tree nearby, we were alone in the rice fields. Little did I realize that this humble structure, nestled among the rice paddies, was the best home I would have for several years.

I never gave up my determination to be free again, but it was impossible to keep from asking What is next? For life was already harsh and joyless, and we were living under unbending discipline. All aspects of city life had been completely destroyed. Kampuchea had become a nation of desperate individuals—disoriented, penniless, without property, and organized into one vast labor camp.

To reach the common toilet facilities from our little home, we had to walk along the dikes separating the rice paddies, then we climbed a short ladder to reach the front door, for the bathroom was about a yard above the ground. Steel drums underneath caught the waste, which was emptied into the rice paddies the next day. Very few of the village people had any knowledge of germs. As a result, many people took ill because they drank the contaminated water in the rice paddies.

At the village meeting, we were told that Prince Sihanouk had returned to Cambodia as head of the Kampuchean government. This news made us feel better, for the prince had ruled Cambodia, on and off, for almost 30 years. We hoped that living conditions would improve. But it did not work that way. The announcement was just a propaganda trick. We were still living under the ruthless rule of unscrupulous leaders. Again and again the question raced through my mind Will it ever change so we can be free again?

Before we reached our new village, Father made a suggestion that was calculated to protect By from being drafted to work in a girls' commune away from home. The Khmer Rouge were following the pattern of taking unmarried children and youth away from the family and away from the village, but married ladies and widows were not usually taken away.

Father suggested that *By* and Sokhom pretend to be married. They were not to live together, but as far as the village leader was concerned they were to be known as husband and wife. This, Father was sure, would keep *By* at home. It worked; she did not have to leave the village.

October 1975

The village of Andong Cheng and its work projects were controlled by the local village leader. Other projects in the area were run by the national government, which secured work crews by drafting young people from the villages. Letine was caught in this draft when actually I was on the list.

In the course of her new work, she witnessed the brutal behavior of the Khmer Rouge. A girl whom she knew was taken out and strangled because her father had been an officer in the army of the former government. It frightened Letine, because our father had also been an official of the former government. Would she be next? Soon after, the Khmer Rouge buried alive a Chinese girl. Letine never did find out the official reason for this killing, but everyone suspected it had to do with the fact that her father had been a businessman before April 1975.

On another occasion, several of the girls went into the woods after lunch to look for plants that could supplement their scanty food supply. Instead of finding food, they found the decomposed bodies of men and women who had been dumped among the trees. No one dared discuss this gruesome find openly, but the news spread quietly among the girls. It was a grim reminder of reality. The Khmer Rouge were killers.

The methods used by the Khmer Rouge in their brutal killings were common knowledge. In order to save bullets, they would often bury a girl alive or bury her up to her neck, allowing her to die slowly of starvation, dehydration, and exposure. Other methods included slashing her throat or beating her on the back of the neck with a hoe handle. Life or suffering meant absolutely nothing to these men who seemed to delight in finding new ways to cause excruciating pain while slowly ending the life of their innocent victims.

In bringing back slavery, starvation, torture, and killing, the Khmer Rouge were reverting to the less enlightened days of Cambodia's history. At times it seemed they were trying to outdo the cruelty practiced in the nation several hundred years earlier.

Love and romance can be engrossing under normal circumstances, but like others things, it was perverted by the Khmer Rouge. Romance among young people was strictly prohibited, but that did not stop boys and girls from being attracted to each other. The leader of Letine's group fell in love with a young man who was working with her. They were never together except at work and even then were extremely careful about their actions. For all they knew, their love for each other remained a secret between them. In an unexpected way this young lady learned that the authorities knew of her affection. Immediately she pretended to be very sick and urgently requested to be sent back home. Each girl knew the reason for her sudden departure. Many lovers who did not have official permission were killed.

When the young lady left, the mantle of leadership fell on Letine. For several months it was her task to struggle with the problems of girls getting sick, feeling they were possessed by devils, or being bothered by the spirits. She also had to select the girls to be sent to different work projects. All this was in addition to her regular work schedule. Before long, an order came for a certain number of girls, which Letine found impossible to fill without including herself.

Her new project turned out to be the hardest yet. Each day they trudged out to the rice paddies before sunrise and continued working there until one hour before midnight. For more than four long months, she harvested during the day and repaired dikes at night, under the floodlights, with only short breaks for food. As the rainy season approached, the

Khmer Rouge cut back on Letine's food, which produced a kind of night blindness that allowed her to see only what was directly in front of her eyes.

The problems Letine faced of girls feeling they were possessed by devils or bothered by the spirits was not strange in Kampuchea. Although the nation was largely Buddhist, this did not keep the people from becoming involved with spirits and demons. Both rich and poor were affected. It was reported that even Prince Sihanouk, before making a decision relating to foreign affairs, made a practice of consulting a medium who claimed to seek advice from the spirits.

Cambodian folklore is filled with requirements to be followed in dealing with the spirits. Failure to appease them, according to the myths, could cause serious trouble. As a result, when problems strike a family, they usually attempt to pacify the spirits.

Buddhist leaders were also involved in spirit worship. Each year the bonzes led out in a special Buddhist festival that included offerings and prayers to the spirits. Some Cambodian parents felt that at childbirth threads must be tied around the wrists and ankles of a new baby to prevent the spirits from escaping the baby's body. When children became sick, parents often gave them strange new names to mix up the spirits thought to be responsible. Special precautions were also taken at the time of death to protect the living from the spirits.

One method of protecting themselves from the spirits, according to their traditions, was to wear a *katha* or good luck charm. Certain precautions had to be observed when wearing the katha. Walking under a house on stilts or walking in front of the home of a prostitute would anger the spirits. When the wearer used the bathroom, the katha must be laid aside. No need to worry about someone stealing it, for the new owner would be in serious trouble with the spirits.

After Letine was drafted by the national government, they kept moving her around. If she had not been injured in a minor accident, my parents might have completely lost track of her. As she was climbing a ladder while leaving a water hole, her foot slipped and she slid down to the lower step. This caused a break in the skin of her leg. The bruise bled and turned black and blue. Infection set in, and soon Letine was unable to work. To help her the leader decided to use an old Cambodian method of healing. A pain in the leg required burning the leg with a stick of lighted incense. Letine knew this would not help, plus it would hurt, so she begged them not to burn her. In its place they gave her some kind of paste made of plants and herbs, but it was useless.

Gradually the pain crept up her leg, causing excruciating agony when she attempted to walk. As if to test her walking ability, a big black snake slithered into her hut. Letine jumped and ran, but when the snake disappeared it was next to impossible for her to get back on her mat even with the help of several girls.

Weeks later the medical man arranged for some penicillin. It reduced the infection, and in a short time she was able to walk again. Feeling better, Letine decided to go to the hospital. I know this sounds strange, but in Kampuchea it was dangerous to go to the hospital alone without a relative or a friend to help.

At the mention of a hospital, Westerners envision a clean medical facility where everything possible is done to help restore health. But this was not the case under the Khmer Rouge. Most hospitals were old, bug-infested school buildings with dirt floors and without modern medicines.

The staff consisted of girls between the ages of 12 to about 18, who were given a four-week course on care for the sick. As a result, the young girls gave very little medical care other than dispensing food and medicine concocted according to old lore. The medicine usually contained roots, leaves, flowers, and carbon mixed with a little sugar and something to hold the ingredients together so it could be molded into little balls. This folk remedy was supposed to cure all kinds of diseases, alleviate the results of accidents, and ease childbirth. *Newsweek* magazine gave a good description of Khmer

Rouge medical care. "The sick must rely on untrained medics who treat cholera with Pepsi-Cola and typhoid with coconut milk" (January 23, 1978, p. 37).

Some of the old remedies seemed to have limited medical benefits; others were useless. For a headache, upset stomach, or general malaise, it was not uncommon to see a Cambodian mother rubbing the back of a child with the edge of a coin. The rubbing continued again and again in the same place with the help of some kind of oil or lubricant so the coin would move easily over the skin. This process was kept up until the skin became red but not broken. The same treatment was often applied to different parts of the body, such as on the chest or abdomen.

For malaria the sick ate *sleng* seeds, which contained a quinine-like substance. There was one real problem with this cure. It was difficult to determine the strength of the quinine-like substance in the seed. If it was very strong, it killed rather than cured. As a result, many sick people died, and some Cambodians used it to commit suicide.

Charcoal from burnt food was used for dysentery, also for infections. To prevent a spear or bullet from penetrating the skin, the people took a concoction made from excrements of a red vulture, parts taken from a dried python, and water. Pregnant women ate the ash from a roasted bat.

Letine found the injections given to her at the Kampuchea hospital a terrifying experience. When the nurse-girl came with a Pepsi bottle full of a red liquid and covered by a dirty plastic top, Letine was horrified. In preparation for the vitamin B_{12} injection, the girl rubbed Letine's arm with cotton, and then picked up a needle, which had been sterilized, and filled the syringe. But before injecting the needle into Letine's arm, she wiped it off with the same cotton she had previously used on Letine's arm. Afraid of a serious infection, Letine decided to have the injection in her left arm.

While real medical care was missing at the hospital, the stay there did provide rest from the dawn-to-dusk work program and a little extra food. After a couple of weeks, Letine's leg was much better. But the infection had not left entirely, and she knew it would require more than rest and food to clear it up. Letine wanted to go home to Father so he could help her.

Recognizing Letine's problem, Father set out to get penicillin from his sister. This sounds simple, and it would have been under normal conditions, for she lived only a morning's walk away. But these were not normal times. Father would miss work. Also he might meet spies or a yotear on the road and be required to show travel papers. At the other village there was always the chance of being seen by the wrong person. If he eluded all other problems, there was danger involved in securing the needed medicine, for my aunt had to buy it on the black market. It was necessary to find someone with the penicillin and bargain for it with gold or jewelry. Fortunately, the medicine was found without difficulty, and the welcome penicillin helped control the infection.

December 1975

Sokhom, the young man Father allowed to join our family, was sent out of the village to work in a fishing project. While he was away some ideas that had been forming in his mind began maturing and demanding action. For a number of months, he and By had been pretending they were married. Several years before, in Phnom Penh, she had been his girlfriend. He thought a great deal of her at that time and still did. His feelings had developed to the place that it was not just a matter of liking her—he had fallen in love with her. She was a beautiful girl, with dark brown eyes, an enticing smile, and a good family. He was sure she would make a good wife. So why not stop the pretending?

Normal Cambodian customs called for the parents to arrange for the marriages of their children, but this would be impossible because Sokhom's father was dead, and he had been unable to locate his mother. And expressing his love for By to the village leader might cost him his life, maybe hers.

Before Sokhom arrived home from the fishing project, he

had completed his planning and had worked out his strategy. Under the circumstances, Father would be the one to consult about his desires, but Sokhom was afraid to start with Father. He needed support. Confiding with Mother would be easier. If she agreed with him, that would be wonderful, and if she would go with him to see Father, that would be better yet.

Getting up his courage and finding the right time for talking to Mother was hard, but he finally told her secretly of his love for *By* and of his desire to marry her. He told her that he was able to take care of her, that he would protect her, and that he would be a good husband. Mother willingly gave her approval. Then Sokhom requested her to accompany him when he talked to Father. She was willing, even willing to talk to Father alone. Father gave his approval but did not want them to start living together before some kind of celebration. They decided there was not much they could do other than have a special meal for the bride and groom and then declare them married.

The date was set, Sokhom, Mother, and *By* went to work planning and getting things ready for the big occasion. It all had to be a secret carefully guarded by the family. Sokhom went into Battambang, took down an old empty house, and brought back the lumber. The little home he built near ours was small, about the size of a bedroom.

From a neighbor Mother borrowed two stones for grinding rice into flour, which she then made into a dough. From another neighbor she borrowed a utensil for making spaghetti-like rice. The dough was put into it and forced through the small holes into boiling water. Sokhom had brought back some fish and dried snakes. This was the special meal for the wedding of Sokhom and *By* on Saturday, December 27, 1975, when they had their little banquet and Father declared them to be husband and wife.

A honeymoon was impossible, even a day off from work was out of the question. The best that could be done was for *By* to move from our little home to the new one Sokhom had built. The next morning they went to work as usual.

Rules about marriage had changed when the Khmer Rouge came to power. Plural marriages had been permitted in Cambodia before that time, but one wife was the rule for most Cambodians. The average Cambodian man did not make enough money to support two or more wives.

In creating a "classless society," the Khmer Rouge found it necessary to do away with many customs that affected our family. As a result, married people were not permitted to show love to each other or to the children. Even pet names between husband and wife such as darling, honey, or sweetheart were forbidden. When children and youth were taken away from their parents, neither were to show any sorrow or sadness. To the Khmer Rouge the family was useless, and they used every possible means to break it up. Children were taken from their parents at a very young age and not allowed to return home. The strength that comes from the love of a family threatened their power and control.

Bad news was always circulating. This time it was about an official of the Khmer Rouge who was reported as saying it was possible to rebuild the nation without the help of the men from the cities. They could be eliminated. He was talking about the "new people," who had been driven from their homes.

We also learned that all the people in Kampuchea more than 12 years of age on April 1975, were to be killed so that no one would have a memory of the past days of the nation. If these rumors turned out to be true, it would do away with all but one or two of our family.

We had no newspapers. The only sources of information were the Khmer Rouge radio, the leader, and rumors. It wasn't long before we found that rumors were usually as reliable—sometimes more so—as the radio or the leader.

January 1976

Harvesttime was always welcome, with its additional rice. On one occasion, rations were actually increased to three cans a day per person, causing everyone to gain a little weight. It was great, but it did not last long. Once the harvest was over, all quotas were cut to one half can of uncooked rice per day.

Under the circumstances, saving rice for the lean seasons was impossible. Even if it could have been stored, very little would have been saved. Each person was desperately hungry. Our physical craving for food was so strong that it overruled any thoughts we might have had of saving rice for a future time. Under such desperate conditions, it's difficult to think rationally.

All children, seven years and older, were required to work. Leang, my 9-year-old brother, was forced to collect 22 pounds of manure each morning. A typical boy, he was always happy to find a fresh pile containing extra water.

Usually his day was divided into two parts, morning work and afternoon school. His classes included Khmer Rouge songs and teachings. Also great importance was placed on hating the capitalist and the need for children to spy on their parents and report to the leader. When this happened, the leader always accepted the word of the children over that of the parents. Very little, if any, emphasis was put on reading and writing.

Most of my work had something to do with rice. The most frightening part of it was the bloodsucking leeches that constantly attached themselves to us in some rice paddies. There were small and large ones. The more blood they sucked, the larger they became.

Working under the cold, adverse conditions of winter or in the scorching sun of summer would have been much easier if the leader had expressed a little appreciation for my work. But that never happened. Not once did I see a smile, a nod of the head, or any kind of gesture indicating thanks or praise. If they said anything, it was in the way of criticism.

Whether we were planting or harvesting, the leader always insisted on everyone working until sunset, and no one complained. To do so would quickly be diagnosed as *chhoeu sattek*, memory sickness. This disease had very obvious symptoms. Anyone talking about the good old days of the past or wishing they would return had a serious case of memory sickness. Other symptoms included complaining about the harsh work, lack of food, sore feet, or the cold rain. Claiming to be sick to avoid work was a very serious case of memory sickness. Those who had continual memory sickness were usually executed. The fear of being accused of this dreaded ailment caused us to continue working without complaint seven days a week, in fact every day of the year.

But at least I was still alive. There were plenty of things to complain about, but according to the reports, there was an increasing number of people who couldn't complain. They had been drowned in the Mekong River. The stories indicated that these people had been ordered to pack their belongings and travel west where there was more rice. Small groups were loaded into boats to cross the river. In the middle of the great river the yotear suddenly turned on the trapped travelers, clubbing them and forcing them overboard. Stories like this, which were constantly circulating, made me thankful to be alive.

I was never much of a singer but By liked to sing. It was always encouraging to hear the old Cambodian songs, but they too were disappearing. The old traditional songs of love, family, country, and religion were banned. Music was now used as a political tool for brainwashing.

The contrast between the old and new melodies was striking. The old melodies were soft and romantic, but the new songs were just the opposite—harsh and rigid. Many times the new music was piped over loudspeakers to the entire village at all hours of the day and night. On a few occasions, the Khmer Rouge used speakers capable of reaching out to the rice paddies.

Evening meetings were all pretty much the same. Very few passed without someone reminding us of the Khmer Rouge slogan: "To keep you alive is no benefit to us, and to let you starve is no loss." No matter how boring the meetings were or how long they lasted—sometimes two or three hours—no one dared close his or her eyes. It would be considered sleeping, a "criminal" offense. Most meetings ended with the leader shouting, "Long live Kampuchea." In response, the whole group would jump to its feet and shout, "Long live Kampuchea."

The *chlops* or informers of the Khmer Rouge were everywhere listening and watching, trying to keep the leaders abreast of the actions and conversation of the workers. These boy spies, usually between 13 and 20 years of age, were brainwashed to give total obedience to the Khmer Rouge. They attempted to mingle with the workers, listening to the conversations. Anyone talking about escaping, expressing disgust with the leadership, or talking about the past was reported immediately and could expect a one-way walk to the woods. Most of the time I could spot the chlops as they eased up to our group, but it was necessary to be constantly on guard.

April 1976

Seven months after we moved into the humble house Father built, we were forced to move a short distance to a new area that had no regular name, so it became known as the New Village. When the eating area had been constructed, certain individuals were designated as cooks. During the same move, the village leader confiscated all pots, pans, and other kitchen utensils for use in the commune kitchen, all except one large pot for boiling water. This arrangement brought new controls and hardship. While it was permissible to boil water in our hut, we could not cook rice. The village leader enforced this rule by checking huts where smoke appeared.

Slowly the New Village became a commune in every detail. Private property was confiscated, and everything belonged to the community. Gradually the boys were assigned to their own work groups, then the girls. Commune living gave the Khmer Rouge greater control over the people. Every day was regimented. The village leader told us when to get up in the morning, when to work, when to attend meeting, when to eat, what to eat, and the kind and color of clothes we were to wear, which was always black. The only things we were allowed to have personally were sleeping mats, mosquito nets, and the clothes we could put in a packsack.

Commune living brought me a serious problem, one I had not experienced before but knew existed. The living quarters were crawling with fleas and lice. Chemicals were not available to combat the little pests. Father boiled my clothes and bedding, but it did not help. I found that a very fine-toothed comb would get a few lice out of my hair, but enough of the little creatures were left to keep the population booming.

With the commune in full operation, Mother and Father were the only ones living in the hut originally built as our home. Father at age 54 and Mother, 51, were considered old people and were assigned to one of three groups of old folks in the village. Each was required to eat and work with his or her own group.

All religious activity was forbidden. Anything to do with Buddhism, Kampuchea's traditional religion, was made a "crime" and punishable by death. Bonzes were forced to endure torture; many were killed. The sacred pagodas of Buddhism were turned into prisons, rice warehouses, or sleeping areas. Some were destroyed. Others were dismantled, stone by stone, to build structures for the Khmer Rouge. The statues of Buddha were either destroyed or disfigured. Buddhist temple bells, which Kampucheans were accustomed to hearing in the dark hours of the early morning, were silent. The black cloud of control had descended on the nation, shutting off all religion as far as outward practice was concerned.

Saturday, April 17, 1976

One year after we had been pushed out of our home in Phnom Penh, the Khmer Rouge celebrated the first anniversary of victory. It was also their New Year's Day. In the meeting that evening, the leader talked about the great deeds accomplished by the Khmer Rouge. But for me it was different. Now I understood why the people I saw near the river, one year ago, looked like walking skeletons.

The Khmer Rouge were celebrating, but the people they were holding in bondage were suffering, slowly dying. On the other hand, there were two good things connected with all the jubilation—extra food for everyone and one day off from work. A little later a change did come that provided one day of rest every tenth day. It was not a new calendar, just a nine-day work and one-day rest schedule.

About this time By and her husband escaped to my aunt's village, where they were accepted. The move enabled them to have more food, but they were still under the heartless cruelty of the Khmer Rouge. In her new village By personally witnessed a Khmer Rouge court trial. The wife of a party member had fallen in love with a married man who was not a member of the Khmer Rouge party. In time, the couple was caught together and accused of adultery. Several days later a meeting of the entire village was called to decide their fate.

The accused were forced to stand before the people, the leader taking his place beside them. Speaking in a matter-of-fact way, he proceeded to tell the details about their love affair, how they were caught in adultery, and that such action was against the laws of the Khmer Rouge. He went on for some time, explaining the strict rules of the Khmer Rouge in this area of conduct and how evil these actions were. At last he got to the penalty, death. Then he asked the accused woman's husband to speak.

Being a member of the Khmer Rouge party, the husband agreed with the comments of the village leader. He then went on and on in his condemnation of his wife for getting involved with the other man. He ended his rambling speech by agreeing that each should die.

The village leader then asked the wife of the man involved to come forward and speak. She refused. Friends knew the reason. She wanted to forgive her husband and have him back, but she did not dare say this in front of the leader.

During the entire proceedings, the little two-and-a-half-year-old boy of the condemned man kept calling for his daddy. His tearful calls could be heard by all. The boy's mother struggled to hold back her tears so she would not be condemned for being against the leader's death decree. Others also struggled with their emotions as they heard the boy calling for his daddy, realizing that soon he would not have a daddy.

No vote was taken. The Khmer Rouge do not work in that way. They state the case and decide the punishment. Then, if no one objects, they take silence as agreement with their decision. In this case, no one objected. No one dared object. No one ever objects in such meetings. Anyone objecting would have been condemned to death. With this forced unanimous death sentence, the accused were marched back to the jail. Several days later they were taken out and clubbed to death.

When the Khmer Rouge came to power, our family was in good health. This continued even under the severe hardships we endured. Much of the credit for our good health was due to my father's knowledge of health and how to care for sickness. But things were changing, and not for the best.

Previously Father had required us to boil all drinking water at home or in the field. At work each family member carried a little pan for this purpose. This procedure was a lot of trouble, because we had to pull rocks together to make a stove, gather sticks, and get a fire going. But by following his instructions, we escaped sickness caused by contaminated water. Now, all our pots and pans were taken by the village leader except the big one in the hut.

In the rice paddies, we had watched others scoop up a handful of water and drink it. Now we were forced to do the same, knowing full well that many people used the paddies as their bathroom. Dysentery soon devastated our family in plague-like fashion. This, plus the starvation diet, severely weakened us. My menstrual periods stopped. It soon became almost impossible for me to keep working.

June 1976
The attempt to establish a new 10-day schedule came to an abrupt end after a short time. The extra rest and the few

times additional food was distributed had helped make my miserable life a little more tolerable. Very few people, however, took part in the sports that were planned for these special days because everyone was too weak.

September 1976

During the monsoon season of 1976, I was faced with the cruel prospect of starving to death. The food service at the village eating area stopped. Each family was forced to find its own food. Our survival depended upon trading, stealing, how much we could get from my aunt, and how much we could find in the countryside. Mother wore a hidden belt in which she carried Thai money. She also had some gold and jewelry. Defying travel restrictions, one or two of us would sneak out to another village in hopes that we could trade with the wife of the leader. She was usually plump, well fed, and willing to give a small bowl of uncooked rice for a piece of jewelry. Such trips were few as our supply of gold and jewelry was limited.

Whenever any of us returned with a little bowl of rice, I couldn't help thinking of the promises the Khmer Rouge made. They were going to create a classless society. Everyone would be equal. There would be no one with plenty of rice while someone else went without. Yet starvation was taking its toll in our village and in many others. Thousands starved while the leaders had plenty to eat.

The Khmer Rouge system required each village to be self-sufficient in food production. In addition, each village was required to supply the national government with a certain quota of rice, which they turned around and exported to earn foreign currency. If the village leader did not manage his rice program in such a way as to provide a good harvest, it was the people who suffered. The national government always received its regular share, and the leader and his family ate well, so the workers received the rest, which that year in our village was almost nothing.

My aunt was very helpful. One of the family would leave home, pretending to leave for work but actually sneaking through the countryside to my aunt's village. With her supply of gold and jewelry, she was able to trade on the black market. Hiding at her place during the day, we would leave for home about midnight, carrying as much rice, oranges, dried fish, corn, and potatoes as possible. Usually we would arrive back in our village during the dark hours of the next morning. The distance between the two villages was not great—only a four or five hour walk for a healthy person. But our weakened condition limited the number of trips we could make. Even though we carried back as much as possible, it was not enough for a starving family of eight.

On one occasion, our village leader passed out the brown powder that comes off the rice during husking and is usually fed to the pigs. We ate it. In fact we ate anything and everything. This included roots, leaves, bamboo shoots, banana plant shoots, and any other kind of greens we could find. Also we ate snakes, rice field mice, ants, ant eggs, water snails, lizards, crabs, and anything else that would provide a little protein. No matter how hard we searched the countryside for extra food, slowly cold, stark starvation was setting in. We knew it, but could do nothing to stop it.

Late one afternoon as I returned with an empty basket despite having searched for several hours for food, I saw some wild rice growing near a rice paddy. This little grain is called "rice," but it is not really a rice product, just a weed. After gathering all the wild rice, I realized this was nothing compared to what we needed in our famished condition.

Just across the dike, not more than 30 feet away, stood a new crop of rice. Most of it still green, yet scattered here and there were a few stocks beginning to ripen. Seeing this food was more than I could stand. My gastric juices began flowing. Resisting my hunger pangs became impossible. Without further thought, I made a quick check to see if anyone was around. No one was in sight. Slipping into the rice paddy, I began gathering both green and partly dried rice as fast as possible. Very soon I had collected enough for a good meal for the whole family.

Just then a sound startled me. Whirling around, I saw a Khmer Rouge guard just reaching the ground from his hideout in a tree. The sight of him froze me in my tracks. Slowly he walked over, looked into my basket, and took it. Then he marched me off to a side room in a house near the center of the village.

It upset me when he left the door open and walked away. I didn't understand his motives and did not go near the door for fear he might be testing me. When I did not return home on time, Father started looking for me and found me in the leader's house. He stood near the open door, for a long time just looking at me, tears streaming down his face. He knew I was in serious trouble, but said nothing. I cried too, but did not speak. We were both petrified of what might follow. Quietly he slipped away, for there was nothing he could do but hope for the best.

Mine was a major "crime," and I knew it. It was not uncommon for people to be executed for stealing food, but I did not really care. The way things were going, death was not far off for all of us. The effects of starvation had already weakened me to such an extent that I felt half dead. I wanted to live, but it would be a relief just to be free from the terrible hunger and suffering.

The night that followed was long, and sleep was impossible. I was all alone with my thoughts and fears, positive I would be killed the next day. Morning came and I could hear people in the other part of the house. Each sound signified the end in my thinking. When a lady brought me a little food, I was shocked. Why were they feeding me when death was just a few hours away? The second night was even longer than the first, and every sound caused my whole body to stiffen. I was sure someone was coming to get me and end it all.

The second day was the longest of my life. Every moment was agonizing. Again they brought me a little food, puzzling me even more. Late in the afternoon a man came to the door and indicated that I should step outside. I was certain that this was the end. The man would take me out to the forest, club me to death, or force me to dig a hole and put me in it and fill in the dirt up to my neck. Whatever the method, I would never come back. Terribly frightened, but resigned to my fate, I slowly stood and walked to the door. Tears poured down my cheeks.

Life was precious, and I was afraid of death. But my only real regret was that I could not say goodbye to my Father and Mother. If only they were nearby, if only I could see them just once more, it would have been easier to face death. Reaching the door, I stopped just inside the room. The man indicated I should come outside. Stepping slowly through the door, I saw the sun setting in the west, a positive sign of my doom.

With head bowed and tears dripping from my chin, I stood before the man and trembled from head to foot. There was total silence for several long moments before he spoke. Then, instead of ordering me to start walking toward the woods, he proceeded to give me a lecture about stealing. This rice, he said, was the people's rice. I was stealing from the people. I was a thief. He made his point time after time. After each one, I bowed, agreeing with him, admitting my wrong deed, and tearfully promising not to do it again. Then, to my surprise, he indicated I could go home. Shocked and confused I stood there, uncertain what to do, not even sure I was hearing him correctly. Raising his voice he said, "Go home." Running home, I collapsed into the arms of my mother. She tenderly held me while my whole body shook.

Every day I lived in constant fear that it would be the end. Time after time as I saw the village leader, I expected trouble. At every evening meeting, I was terrified, thinking he would use the occasion to make a public example of me. For weeks I lived in constant terror that each day would be my last.

Death was on every side. Morning after morning the burial processions slowly moved through the village and out to the little cemetery near the rice paddies. The dead body was wrapped in an old, dirty, patched garment, and was carried on bamboo sticks. There were no religious leaders to help. But in spite of the threats against religion, desperate individuals sought comfort in their faith. The need for help was so powerful that many of the starving risked everything by openly worshiping at a Buddhist altar.

Newborn babies had little chance of surviving. At the last when there was no hope, peasant healers were usually called in to work their magic and appease the spirits. The baby was given a special drink made from leaves and roots. Then they would stand around the little one as they chanted and sang to drive the spirits away. But not long after, the parents were usually seen carrying their precious little bundles out to the graveyard.

Some desperately hungry people resorted to cannibalism. Instead of the Khmer Rouge providing food for these famished workers, they were tortured in the most brutal manner.

At the evening meeting, after repeating his usual slogans, the leader took time to warn us against catching and eating crabs or fish while we worked in the rice paddies. It took time from our tasks, he said, and angkor, the higher organization of the Khmer Rouge, did not approve of such actions. He said we were stealing time from angkor and that it would not be tolerated. Near the end of the meeting, the leader told his starved listeners that they must develop a joy in working for and serving the Khmer Rouge.

At another meeting, during the darkest days of starvation, the village leader had the diabolic courage to remind us in his closing remarks that our lives meant nothing to the Khmer Rouge. As we went home from the meeting, with hardly enough strength to walk, the leader's words kept ringing in our ears, "To keep you alive is of no benefit to the Khmer Rouge, to allow you to die is no loss."

Families with marital problems fought over food because the wife or husband would hide it from the other. Fortunately, our family supported each other. We shared our food, always working as a family unit to preserve our existence.

In our desperation, we decided that we must escape to my aunt's village. Once before that same village leader had rejected us, but all of us wanted to try again regardless of the consequences. We felt certain we would die if we stayed in our village and reasoned that it made little difference where we died—in our village, in another, or as we tried to escape. We had everything to gain and nothing to lose.

October 1976

As a first move, Father sent Sarith to let my aunt know we were coming. A few days later he sent the rest of the family while he stayed behind and continued working. After about a week he left too. Sarith was accepted, but the village leader refused us, ordering our arrest. Yotear quickly hustled us off to a holding camp for escapees. Day after day we were shifted from one place to another, always under guard. Each night the boys' legs were tied so they could not escape. A week later we were forced to walk back to our village. Just as we arrived Father was leaving. He thought we had been accepted, so he had given away the few things we owned and had eaten the last few grains of rice.

Now our problems were compounded. We were back in a village that had no rice, our own rice containers were completely empty, our supply of items to trade was very low, and the village leader knew that we had tried to escape. To add to our predicament, Letine's leg began giving her trouble. At night she suffered severely, so much so that it seemed the pain would drive her insane. Yet we had nothing to ease the pain or fight the infection. Night after night, the dreadful ordeal continued, causing a terrible mental strain on each of us. The starvation and Letine's pain were almost more than we could endure.

Father wanted to make another trip to my aunt's village to get penicillin, but he was afraid to try. We were being watched because of our attempt to escape. So Father did the best he could by searching for healing herbs in the woods. Letine ground them up and placed them on her infected leg three times a day. In addition, she kept the wound clean by bathing it with warm water. After a number of weeks, the pain gradually eased, and eventually the leg healed.

Somehow we managed to stay alive until the rice harvest

in December. I can't explain how or why we survived, because there were many days when I did not expect to see the next morning. People were dying all around us. Our stomachs were bloated, our ribs showed, and we were extremely weak. Nevertheless, we were alive and very thankful, for thousands upon thousands did not live to see the new harvest.

March 1977

One evening, after we had harvested rice all day, a strong, demanding knock at the door of our hut startled us. When Father opened it, he found the village leader standing there with a stern look on his face. He had never visited us before. In a brief but authoritative manner, he told Father to prepare to leave early the next morning for a work project outside the village, then he left. It was a strange order, because Father was classified as an old man, and so had never been required to go away from the village on work projects.

As I reflected on the leader's stern order, I suddenly remembered Father's former position as a government leader. For nearly two years our family had zealously guarded this secret to protect his life. Had the village leader learned our secret? Was this a plot to get rid of Father? Had our attempt to escape to another village caused the leader to mistrust Father and decide that the village might be better off without him?

The entire family felt better after learning that most of the other men, old and young, were going to the same project. Father tried to calm our fears with this information, but I could not put away the haunting feeling of impending trouble.

There were good reasons for this uneasiness. A few weeks earlier a vicious story had circulated through the village about Father having made decisions in his government work that had hurt the farmers. Actually, he had nothing to do with farms, but the ugly story gave us sleepless nights. Not only was it false, but it also identified Father as a former government leader.

Also Father had difficulty adjusting to his new life as a peasant farmer. His background seemed to shine through the old, patched clothes. He walked erect and talked and acted differently than most of the other men. We were very proud of him, but worried.

Another incident added fuel to our fears. Suddenly the man Father had worked with for many months started working for the village leader. Many times Father and his friend had discussed their plans for escaping. With this new job, his friendship with Father cooled. The leader's visit aroused the fear that Father's former friend might have revealed his plans.

Through the night Father's courage was strong as we talked in whispers. Early the next morning, he was ready to leave. An anxious family gathered at the door to bid him goodbye. As usual, his shoulders were thrown back, his head held high. Watching him walk away was too much for me, and my eyes began blurring as tears sneaked down my cheeks.

Long, anxious days followed without any information. About a week later one of the family overheard a whispered conversation. Someone reported that Father was dead, killed by the village leader. No one mentioned it to us. Hiding our faces and choking back tears, we forced ourselves to continue working, hoping it was just a false rumor. During the agonizing days that followed, we strained our ears to pick up additional news. There was nothing. Sometime during the second week, a few of the men began returning, but no one spoke to us. The whispered conversation could not be proved or disproved. Our suspense for the next three weeks was almost unbearable.

When a distant relative returned, we were sure he would tell us the facts, but instead he avoided us, which only confirmed our worst fears. The slim hope we had seized upon and had held to so tightly disappeared. Our relative was afraid he might get in trouble. Father was dead; we were certain of it. Several days went by before our relative sneaked around to one of the family and confirmed the story.

During the weeks that followed, we shed our tears in secret. Emotions, such as crying, were not tolerated by the Khmer Rouge. All expressions of feeling had to be choked back. No one must see or hear. Mother could show no emotion at her work. She came home, night after night, to weep quietly on her mat. During this time of deep anguish, the leader was spotted walking around our hut, listening to our conversations. He was suspicious of us, and we knew that we could be next.

Father was gone, our hearts were heavy with grief, and our stomachs were just returning to a normal size after the severe spell of starvation, but we were still weak and sick. Now friends avoided us, and the leader was spying on us.

Additional information about Father eventually came from one of his close friends. He told my brother Saat to meet him at the well. There, he confirmed the fact that Father was dead. He said the village leader had told Father he was taking him to an isolated location where he would care for cows. Later the friend watched Father get on the back of the leader's motorcycle and ride with him into the trees. The leader then returned without him. Father was never seen again.

This friend also brought a strange message from Father: "Tell my children to get revenge for me." Get revenge! This was shocking! So unlike Father. All his life he had been a man of peace, never given to violence.

May 1977

After Father's death, we tried once again to escape. We knew that such a move would be extremely dangerous and might cause the leader to arrange for our death. But we had to leave. We could not stay in the same village with the man who had killed Father.

Yotear were waiting for us as we passed beyond our little group of huts. They didn't say so, but it seemed like they knew we were coming. My heart sank. Caught again! Now the village leader would surely have us all killed. I was so

71

frightened it was hard to understand what the yotear were saying. Another shock! Instead of arresting us and marching us back to the village leader, they asked if we wanted to go back to our village or to another. I don't know what they thought of us, because we were all so shocked we didn't know what to say. Such consideration was strange for the Khmer Rouge. In fact, it was one of the few times any kindness was shown by our rulers or the soldiers. We chose the village of Chhong Chhdor because it was near fruit orchards and water for fishing.

June 1977

Leaving our home in the New Village, where Father had been with us, filled me with a mixture of sadness and happiness. I would get more food in the next village, but my eyes watered over again as we said goodbye to the little hut Father had built. It had become special to me since his death and hard to leave. He had built it, and he had been with us when we lived there. It represented his love, his care for his family, but now he was gone. Under the circumstances, we could not even put a marker where he had fallen, but there was a marker etched deep in our memories. It reads: "Huot Eng Pheng, a loving husband and father, who did his best to lead his family to freedom. Killed by the Khmer Rouge village leader, Thursday, March 10, 1977."

In our new village, food was not a big problem. Our rations were small, just enough to keep us alive, but that was many times more than we had received for months in the past. Living was also different. This village was totally devoted to the commune concept. There were no family dwellings, just large huts where a number of people slept. All our meals and other activities took place elsewhere, and our family was divided.

Soon the village leader took Lim to a government rope project. Lim was happy to go because of the good reports about the working conditions. But when he arrived at the project, his hopes shattered. It was a terrible place. Conditions were just the opposite of the rumors floating around. The boys working on the project were pale, skinny, and weak. There were no sleeping quarters—all their mats were on the ground, out in the open. The government had been purposely spreading false information about the working conditions.

On the first day, before daylight, Lim was awakened by the shrill blast of a whistle. Without eating any breakfast, the boys were soon marching in the darkness and stumbling through water about two feet deep. The first rays of light revealed nothing but jute plants standing in the water. This was his new job, getting the jute plants out for making rope and sacks.

Working in the water all day long and in all kinds of weather was more than he could stand. Before long another boy from a village near his decided to join him in escaping. Their enthusiasm to return to their villages was a dreadful mistake, for to get food in the village it was necessary to have your name on the village food list.

Mother did her best to help by sharing with Lim, but the slim portions she received were just enough for one person. If he stayed in the village, both he and Mother would slowly starve to death. After many fruitless discussions in which they tried to devise a way to keep Lim from starving to death while staying in the village, he finally decided that he must return regardless of the consequences. It was the only way to save Mother. Tearfully Mother, Letine, and Leang bade him goodbye. They felt sure they would never see him again.

Back in camp Lim immediately talked to the man in charge of his work group, a stranger to him, but a man from his own village. He told Lim neither he nor the government leader had known he was missing. Then Lim heard some of the sweetest words ever to reach his ears. His group leader said he would report his absence in such a way that there would be no trouble for him.

November 1977

Saat and I worked for only a short time in another rope project before being assigned to a national government construction team building a dam. In this project three crews were kept working around the clock. Instead of working eight-hour shifts, each person worked two four-hour shifts in each 24 hours.

Day or night, rain or shine, we carried heavy loads with our strong bamboo pole supporting a basket at each end. The loads were so heavy I could not walk more than a few yards before becoming exhausted and having to put the baskets down for a rest. These stops were brief, because a work leader was usually lurking nearby and demanding I move on. The heavy loads totally sapped my strength. My shoulders ached and my back hurt, but the work continued every day of the week.

One evening an exhausted group of girls attempted to run away, but were caught by the guards, who promptly marched them back to camp. Since some of the girls were my friends, the leader presumed I had accompanied them. No matter how hard I tried, I could not convince her otherwise. Punishment consisted of cutting our food supply and assigning extra working hours.

February 1978

The continuous heavy loads drained every ounce of my strength. In that condition, feelings won out over better judgment. Following an impulsive thought, I made plans to run away and find Mother. The area was strange, and there was real danger of being caught. Also the serious consequences of a second offense frightened me, but in my mind I felt I had no choice. I desperately needed a rest, and I felt that I had to see Mother.

Waiting until late in the afternoon, I started out by moving through the rice paddies to avoid detection. With the help of a full moon, I found Mother's village without trouble, but I learned the disconcerting news that she was another hour away.

Reaching Mother's hut was hard because the moon had set, but it was worth the effort. The visit gave me a good rest, renewing my strength and courage. Back at the dam no one had detected my absence, and I was able to return unnoticed.

A large part of the walk was made at night, but I was not afraid of sexual attacks. Girls were able to walk alone at night without fear. The Khmer Rouge were strict on this issue. If anyone violated the rule, he was endangering his own life. At least this was what the leaders said, and outwardly it was enforced.

Some questions were raised about these high standards when yotear would be seen marching into a village, picking out a young lady, and ordering her to march ahead of them into the woods. She would never be seen again in the village, and it was generally understood that she had been gang-raped then killed.

Just before the dam was completed, a heavy rain fell above another dam up the river, breaking it and sending a wall of water over our dam. The whole area was flooded in a few hours. It surrounded my sleeping quarters, and for a few moments it looked as though I was in for severe trouble, but the crest soon passed, allowing me to escape without harm.

The top leaders of the Khmer Rouge were well educated people. They should have understood that forcing workers to perform their tasks without wages caused people to lose all interest in doing a good job. Some of us who were the slaves could clearly understand the reasons for this disaster and others like it.

More than three years had passed since I had been suddenly driven out of my home in Phnom Penh. Father had managed to position us about four days' walk from the Thai border, but he was gone. Our family was separated, had been assigned to different work projects. Escape, a part of my dreams for months, now seemed impossible. Despair began to dominate my thinking. The future, as far as I could see, was nothing more than days, weeks, months, and years, if I lived, of backbreaking slave labor.

June 1978

Mother always kept track of us children no matter how much we were moved around. She knew Saat was in the hospital and that I was at Otaki working in the rice paddies, so she sent Lim and Leang to give me an urgent message. Mother was being moved. She and the family were to gather at a central loading area the next day, Monday the twelfth. Trucks would transport them to a new village. Not knowing her destination, she wanted me to sneak away immediately and join them so we would not be separated.

The boys arrived late afternoon on the eleventh. The thought of being separated from Mother just about paralyzed me, but making a quick decision at that particular time was impossible. I knew Mother would be hurt, for all my life we had been very close. Yet in my sick, weakened condition I was unable to make a decision. The boys returned home alone. After a restless night, with almost no sleep, I was still undecided. Through the day, while working, I tossed the pros and cons back and forth trying to find an answer.

My health was very poor. Food made me sick and was hard to hold down. Walking was difficult. In addition, I was suffering night blindness, which prevented me from traveling after sunset. The possibility of collapsing along the road haunted me, especially if it was necessary to run while escaping. Under these conditions, I stood a good chance of getting caught and being tortured with the plastic bag treatment. In this punishment they put a plastic bag over the head of an offender to cut off the supply of air. When the "criminal" would fall to the ground, gasping for air, the tormenters would remove the bag just long enough to let the victim get a few good breaths of air, enough to revive him or her. Then the bag would go on again. This torture would be repeated time after time until the person became hysterical. Just the thought of getting caught made me shudder. That kind of treatment would be impossible to endure.

But the thought of staying behind and being cut off from

Mother also terrified me. I would be separated from my family, maybe never to see them again. All morning and into the afternoon the debate in my mind raged. By early afternoon, almost 24 hours late, I made my decision. I would escape. Within minutes, without returning to my quarters, I was walking. Now it was a race against the sun.

Getting there took longer than I expected. The sun was setting as I walked into the village. Mother was leaving on the twelfth, and this was the twelfth, and it was getting dark. Blindness prohibited me from going on, and my cousin, who lived there, informed me that it was useless. Mother had left. Her confirmation of this fact released my tears like breaking a dam. Father was gone; now Mother was gone.

In her kind way, my cousin did everything possible to help me. She gave me a bucket to get water for a shower, but I was so blind I couldn't find the water. Gently, she led me by the hand to the water, the bathroom, and handed me food. Then she led me to a mat, where I spent another sleepless night.

Panic petrified my thinking as I rushed to the loading zone soon after daylight the next morning. Once I arrived there, desperation mixed with anger overwhelmed me. I thought Mother would have waited, but I was too late. She was gone, and no one knew the destination of the truck she was riding on.

While I stood by a tree, looking through my tears at the trucks loading and leaving, the thought of being cut off forever from Mother plunged me into the depths of anguish. How long I stood there submerged in my grief, I don't know. Slowly reality returned.

As I watched the trucks, I was suddenly struck with a new thought, and guilt swamped me. All morning I had been thinking only of myself and the heartache I was suffering. Now I was thinking of my Mother and the pain she was forced to endure because of my actions. I understood very well how much she loved me. It must have caused her terrible distress when she realized I was not coming. In my mind I could see the ordeal she had gone through as she had boarded the truck, knowing there was a good chance she would never see her youngest daughter again. In my imagination I could see her standing up in the back of the truck, longingly looking down the road, tears streaming down her cheeks, still hoping that I would show up at the last minute. But I had failed her. These thoughts were almost more than I could stand.

Despite the desperate loneliness and guilt I was experiencing, a new thought began slowly developing. First in the form of a question. Would it be possible to search and find Mother? After thinking about it for a few moments the answer came. Why not? I had nothing to lose by searching. I might find her. With this new plan came a surge of hope and courage.

As another family boarded a truck, it was easy to pretend I was one of them. The trick worked fine, but soon I realized things were not going well. This truck was heading toward the area I had just left, my work project. Fear gripped me as all kinds of terrifying thoughts raced through my mind. What would happen if the truck stopped, they searched it, and found me, a runaway? The answer was unnerving—the dreaded plastic bag treatment.

Pulling my big hat down over my face, I slipped as far down into the truck as possible. Every time the driver slowed or stopped, my heart seemed to stop. The truck stopped several times during the next few minutes, but each stop was short. After what seemed like hours, I peeked out, happy to find we were past the danger area.

In the late afternoon, the truck stopped near a small village of 15 to 20 grass huts and unloaded the passengers, but Mother was not there. A lady who said she knew Mother informed me she had continued to travel west. Following that information, I was soon walking on the main road leading to Thailand.

One thing I could depend upon, Mother always did baby-sitting, and this was usually done near the center of the village in the big sheltered area where everyone ate. With

Mother's habits in mind, I started searching every village. If it happened to be mealtime, I stopped to eat. With so many people being moved by the national government, the village leaders had no way of checking on me. For all they knew I was one of the official travelers.

Like most of the others, except the leaders, I was barefooted. Blisters soon formed on my feet. But I kept walking, searching every village I could find, but Mother seemed to have vanished. On the second evening, a family said that they knew Mother but that she had been taken in a different direction than I was traveling. The next morning, trying to follow their directions, I checked a number of villages, but when evening came the net results were more blisters and bleeding feet, but no Mother.

Another and another day passed with still more blisters, but no Mother. Walking along the road in the late afternoon of the fifth day, exhausted and desperate, I felt that the setting sun was haunting me, symbolizing my fate. While watching it disappear behind the trees, I cried as I realized that my chances of finding Mother were disappearing along with my time and strength.

That evening a man told me the trucks that had left on the twelfth had gone off the main road to villages out in the country. As I followed his directions, I kept hearing the same story but never found Mother. A boy claiming to be on the same truck with Mother said she had been dropped off at Phnom Touch, a village a good distance behind me. I remembered checking it, but may have missed her. Before going to sleep that night I determined to return to Phnom Touch and search it carefully.

The next day about the time the sun was directly overhead and as I was trudging slowly along, I was overtaken by a man on a tractor pulling a load of rocks. Signaling him, I asked for a ride. He stopped. What a relief it gave me just to rest my legs! Several hours later, arriving at Phnom Touch, I expected the driver to stop, but he kept going. After passing five other villages he finally stopped.

Phnom Touch was a large village with three different commune organizations within its borders, each with its own eating area. The first I found had about a hundred children plus grandmothers, which forced me to take a few minutes to check it thoroughly, but Mother was not in the group. The ladies willingly told me how to find the other two food areas. Hobbling on, I found the next eating area with its children and grandmothers, but no Mother. Only one shelter remained, and I was certain the boy had given me the wrong information. In my despair, I was afraid to check the last one, sure she would not be there. Then, what would I do?

Everything seemed to be crumbling around me. I had no idea what was next. My scant supply of strength was nearly depleted. I was discouraged and all alone, searching without success, cut off from all the people who loved me, and under the control of a system that had no interest in me.

Terrified, I trudged up the little incline to the last eating area. Fear almost prevented me from looking around, but as my eyes adjusted to the shade, nothing could keep me from checking it carefully. It was similar to the other two I had checked, children all over the place and a large number of older ladies, but no— Wait! On the other side, near that large group of children—was that Mother at the edge of the shelter?

It was! She saw me at the same time I saw her. Suddenly I forgot about my blistered, bleeding feet and sore legs. With new energy I moved faster than I had moved for days. As we approached each other, bowing in the traditional Cambodian manner of greeting, torrents of tears flowed down my cheeks, making it impossible for me to speak. But Mother understood.

CHAPTER

September 1978

A few weeks after I located Mother, the attention of the family was diverted from my health to Mother's distress. The village leader accused her of stealing palm sugar. From the stories going around, we learned that someone had attempted to steal sugar from a palm tree near the kitchen. But apparently the person had been scared off, leaving the pan he or she was collecting the sap in under the tree.

The damaging part was the pan, which at one time had belonged to Mother. That was before the leader had confiscated all pans for the kitchen. Everyone in the kitchen knew the pan once had belonged to Mother, so she was automatically guilty of this serious offense. But I knew Mother was not guilty, because it was impossible for her to gather palm sugar from a tall tree.

To accomplish this job a man ties small bamboo cups to his waist, then pulls himself up the tree with his bare hands and feet. Once at the top of the telephone pole-like tree, he uses a safety strap to secure himself so he can work with his hands. Carefully he makes cuts at the base of the flowers, allowing the sap to flow. Then he must attach a bamboo cup under each flower to collect the sap.

Every day he must climb the tree to gather the cups and place others under the flowers. Loaded with these bamboo cups full of palm sugar sap, the man must then slowly inch his way down with his bare hands and feet. After several days, the collected sap is boiled to get rid of the water, with the end product tasting something like brown sugar. Understanding this difficult collection process, I knew it was an impossible task for Mother. Eventually she was able to convince the leader of that fact.

Again the family attention turned to my health. Mother, desperate to find extra food for me, traded a ruby ring for a bowl of rice. But the rice was not enough. A few days later I collapsed, falling face down into the water and mud. Several girls quickly helped me to a sitting position so my head was above the water.

The village hospital, where I ended up, was like the one Letine had been in. It, too, was run by young girls, but I found something Letine had not mentioned. The nurse-girls were not above taking advantage of their hungry, sick patients. One of them offered me three ripe bananas for my only western style bra. My hunger was so severe I took the bananas and would likely have made the trade for just one.

After a few days of rest, I was sent hobbling along the path toward home. Passing a small clearing in the trees, I was surprised to find several children playing. It was a rather unusual sight, for boys and girls seven years and older were expected to be in school or working, and younger children were usually too sick or too listless to play. As I stood there a few minutes, resting and watching, I suffered an attack of nostalgia. My mind went back to my childhood days in Phnom Penh, to the fun we used to have playing hide and seek on the grounds of the pagoda near our home.

As I again began walking, a small red flower attracted my attention. Again my mind went swirling back to Phnom Penh, to the time when we girls would go to market with Mother. There we would see young ladies with bright red fingernails. This always intrigued us, and we had wanted to do the same to our nails, but Mother had always refused to buy the red polish. That's where these little red flowers came in. By taking them apart petal by petal and wetting the petals, we could just fit them over our fingernails, where they would stick for a short time. It had always been so much fun to walk around with our fingernails all red! We would hold our heads high, prancing along and trying to act like the young ladies we had seen at the market.

October 1978

Letine must have drunk some contaminated water, for she suddenly developed a serious case of dysentery and was sent to the village hospital, then on to the big hospital. About this same time, the village leader decided I should go to the big hospital. Mother helped me get down the ladder from our sleeping quarters, but I could walk no farther. Four ladies carried me on bamboo poles to a waiting "ambulance"—a truck. Sitting in the back of that Khmer Rouge "ambulance," I traveled seven and a half miles on what once had been a nice highway, but in recent years it had been neglected by the government and was full of potholes. The driver, I am sure for his own comfort, attempted to miss as many of the holes as possible, but there were many he could not avoid. For me, in the back of that truck-ambulance with its hard springs, it seemed like the roughest road I had ever traveled on. Arriving at the hospital exhausted and battered from bouncing around on the steel truck bed, I just remained in the truck until some girls came with a bamboo stretcher and carried me inside.

In some ways the big hospital, one of their best, was better than the little hospital near our village. Yet it was crude compared to Western standards. Like the others, it was crawling with bugs, and filth was everywhere. They did, however, have a limited amount of real medicine, and the food was better.

Weakness forced me to stay in bed on the three-inch slats of wood with a two-inch space between. The condition of my feet and legs, along with the hard slats of the bed, caused a great deal of pain, and there was no medicine to relieve it.

Thinking they would take me to the village hospital, Mother went there but was shocked and a little confused when she could not find either of her girls. Determined to find us, she walked the seven and a half miles to the big hospital. Naturally, I was surprised to see her, but her visit was more than a mere call. It was a powerful love tonic. The effect on me was better than all their medicine. It cheered me up, actually causing me to feel better.

The next morning brought another pleasant surprise. Letine walked in. She had reached the big hospital before I had arrived, but we had not found each other. Afraid we might become separated, Mother shared her rings, necklaces, and other jewelry with us. To keep mine safe I sewed a little pocket inside my blouse.

How did I happen to have a needle? Our family usually had a needle or two. Several needles were in the supplies that we picked up as we rushed out of our home in Phnom Penh. Also on one or two occasions, the village leader had distributed needles. It was important for the Khmer Rouge to keep the people in needles so our clothes would last longer.

Thread was the big problem. The little that came from home was soon used up. From then on we secured thread by taking cloth apart one single thread at a time. Then we would put several of these old threads together and rub beeswax on them. If we had new cloth, it made much better thread. We secured the beeswax from some of our relatives.

Even though it took several hours to walk from our village, Mother came often, braving the danger of traveling without permission, determined to keep in close touch with her girls. One time, shortly after I arrived, she was able to bring 10 eggs that she had secured on the black market by trading a small piece of jewelry. The temptation to eat all 10 at once was almost overwhelming. I was so hungry! Each time the young girls came around with their medicine, I searched for the pills that looked like the vitamins Father used to buy. My one chance of getting better was building up my body so it could heal itself.

Near Letine's bed a lady was suffering from a sizable abscess on her hip. It was so deep the young girls put a large bundle of bandages into it each day to absorb the pus and blood. The dirty bandages were then washed without soap, hung out to dry, and used the next day on another patient.

Since Letine was feeling much stronger, she began walking around the hospital. In one large room she found the area a Westerner might call the intensive care unit. Most of the patients in this room were very sick, unable to get out of bed. The floor was dirt. Each bed was made of bamboo slats set about two inches apart. When these seriously ill people needed to relieve themselves, they just let it go, allowing it to fall through the slats to the floor, creating a mound under each bed. Later, one of the girls would cover the pile with a little dirt, increasing the mound. Letine said that the stench was unbearable.

My sister made friends with a young lady whose only relative had just died. Some of the young girls felt sorry for her so gave her extra food. This she shared with Letine, and Letine with me. It was exactly the kind of medicine I needed most, good nutrition, and it did the job. My night blindness cleared up, and gradually the swelling in my legs went down. I began to feel better. Life took on new meaning.

January 1979

The hospital days were long and boring after Letine was discharged. Every day was the same routine, and time seemed to stand still. Under these circumstances, I found it difficult to keep from worrying about the future. Almost four years had passed since we had been driven from our home. As far as I could see, my future had not changed. It held nothing but more hard work under ruthless taskmasters.

The Khmer Rouge had turned their calendar back to zero when they came to power in April 1975. According to them, it was Year Three. Soon, in April, it would be Year Four. But I was still following the Western calendar, which indicated January 1979.

On this particular day, just after the rice was distributed, the nurse-girls started acting peculiar. Instead of the usual activities of the afternoon, they gathered in small groups and talked excitedly. By late afternoon their agitation was obvious. Something was wrong, but I could not determine the reason for their strange actions. That night the news leaked out. The Vietnamese army was invading Kampuchea. Only a few details were available, but what I heard just about took my breath away. The reports indicated that the Vietnamese were moving fast, using jet fighters and tanks, and heading west on National Highways 5 and 6. Phnom Penh had already fallen without a struggle.

I was stunned. My physical condition was a little better, but I was still extremely weak, all alone, and barely able to walk a short distance without help. Now an invading army was coming. During the first part of that night, I desperately tried to find a solution to my predicament. But my thoughts just went in circles. All I could think about was being trapped in a hospital. In the dark hours of the morning, I was surprised to find myself actually feeling happy about the Vietnamese invaders. They might stop the killing and help move the nation back to pre-Khmer Rouge days. By morning I felt torn between the traditional hatred of the Vietnamese and fear of the Khmer Rouge.

Daylight brought another dilemma. The nurse-girls ordered every patient to leave the hospital, causing near panic. It didn't matter how sick we were or whether we could or couldn't walk, the order was the same—get out. My village was seven and a half miles away. Walking without help was absolutely impossible. So it was a real relief when old trucks started arriving to take us to our village hospitals. Once there, I was dismissed immediately.

National Highway 5, running from Phnom Penh through Battambang to the Thai border, was near Mother's village and could easily be seen from her home. During the past four years, cars were infrequent on this and every other road in Kampuchea, but when I arrived at Mother's place, National Highway 5 was carrying more automobiles than any of us had seen for years. They were all headed toward the border. It looked like a parade—big cars, luxury cars, cars covered with branches of trees, all headed in the same direction. The meaning was clear. Leaders of the Khmer Rouge, with their expensive autos, along with diplomats from the embassies in Phnom Penh, were running from the Vietnamese.

Early the next morning our village leader was seen sneaking away through the trees. He, too, was fleeing. Quickly the news spread. Workers began returning to their shacks from the rice paddies and soon were leaving the village. Mother and Letine rushed over to the eating area to look for food, but they were too late. Others had already emptied the rice storehouse. But they did find Mother's old pan. It was good to have it with us again, for it had become a part of our family.

With the help of Mother and Letine, it took considerable time to walk the few blocks to the main road. On National Highway 5, scores of people were heading for the Thai border, the same way the cars were going. With very few others, we bucked the traffic, heading in the opposite direction, toward Battambang. Mother was determined not to allow freedom to separate her family. All the family must be pulled together first, then we could think about heading for freedom.

My slow gait gave my brother Leang plenty of time for exploring. He was only 12 years old at the time, but was performing magnificently, just like a man. Soon, his exploration turned up a cart, and I was told to ride so they could move faster.

A little later he caught five ducks, tied them together with string, and put them on the cart with me. After another kilometer or two, he found a bag of unhusked rice. We were proud of him, but he was not too happy with me, for as we hurried along, the cart hit a pothole, startling me. I jumped and scared the ducks; they jumped, broke the string, and were gone, heading for water. Leang took off after them. The ducks plunged in with Leang in pursuit. The pond was only waist deep, but Leang learned very quickly he was no match for ducks in water.

A little before dark, on the third day, while crossing the

road to get water for a shower, I glanced up and saw a boy coming toward me. He looked familiar. I stood there a moment as he came closer. It was Lim, my brother. He, too, had found a cart and was gathering rice and bananas.

Months had passed since we had seen or heard from him. With the whole population in confusion, we did not know where he had been or, more important, whether he was dead or alive. His appearance on the road to Battambang was a most happy surprise. The story he told made us realize how fortunate we were to have him with us, alive and well.

After leaving Mother's village, he had been placed in a boys' camp and had been forced to work hard on very little food. Desperately hungry, he had stolen a cob of dry corn and had been caught. For this "crime" the Khmer Rouge had placed him in prison at night with about 50 other offenders. Even as a prisoner he had to work during the day, but at night he, with the other "criminals," were placed back in the wooden prison building, where each boy had one leg clamped to the wooden floor, making it impossible to escape.

His prison term had not been up when news of the Vietnamese invasion reached his camp. As the Khmer Rouge leaders were fleeing, he rushed back to the prison to get his mat before leaving for Battambang. Stepping inside the door, he stopped abruptly, shocked by the sight. There before him, scattered around the wooden floor were pools of blood and the mutilated bodies of four boys who had been hacked to death while their one leg was still in the iron clamp. Stunned, Lim slowly backed out, leaving his mat and heading for Battambang. But the battle between the Vietnamese and Khmer Rouge armies prevented him from reaching the road.

In danger of getting killed, he found a secure place to hide. The battle continued for two days, while Lim stayed under cover. Slowly the Vietnamese were able to break the resistance of the Khmer Rouge, and he started out again for Battambang.

When the news first arrived of the invasion, he and most of the boys from the prison had been working in the fields.

Those who had been killed were apparently sick or unable to work for some reason. Just before the Khmer Rouge fled, they must have decided to inflict their last act of torture on those helpless boys.

Lim was emotionally shaken as he relived the horrible picture, still vividly etched in his mind. Almost in a whisper he said, "I could have been one of those boys."

February 1979

After passing the village where we last had seen Father and where we had nearly starved to death, we walked into Battambang. The family was all together again, except for my sister Nakry, her two boys, and my uncle who was taken prisoner by the Khmer Rouge. The city was in confusion. With the Vietnamese controlling, no one knew what to expect next.

Soon after we got located in a big empty house near the river, we checked our food supply and were astounded. The various members of the family had been collecting many different food items, but no one had any idea it amounted to so much. The list included 20 large 100 kilo (220 pounds) sacks of rice, two oxen, one buffalo, several pigs, bananas, coconuts, and various other kinds of fruit. An impressive food supply for people who had been critically hungry just a few days before.

With my older sister and her two boys missing, Mother was restless. Every morning before daylight she left the house for a certain intersection where National Highway 5 and another major road crossed. Hundreds of people passed this corner every day. She hoped Nakry would be one of them. One afternoon I was surprised to see her returning home early, for she usually stayed until it was dark. This was unusual, but the "answers" were following close behind. She had found Nakry and the boys.

In telling how it happened, Mother said she had seen a lady who looked like Nakry carrying a sack of rice on her head. The direction she had been walking made it impossible for her to see her face. Also with so many people surrounding her, Mother could not see if two boys were with this person. Then the lady had turned her head just a little. She was Nakry! Mother started running, pushing through the crowd, calling her name. Catching up, she found Nakry holding each boy's hand.

Looking at Nakry, then at Mother, I could not help thinking of the strength of a Mother's love for her children. Her days of faithful watching at the corner had paid off. Mother was successful in pulling her family together in spite of the difficulties.

Several months went by before it was possible to find some clues indicating the plans of the Vietnamese. Slowly, the picture began developing. They placed a Kampuchean, one they could trust, in charge of the city of Battambang, opened the hospitals, and brought back real doctors and medicine. It seemed for a short time that Kampuchea might be changing back to the Cambodia I once knew. But this was just a happy thought.

News about the new Kampuchean rulers in Phnom Penh was very upsetting. We learned that they had once been with Pol Pot, the former bloodthirsty leader of Kampuchea and that he had lost confidence in them and had ordered their execution. By escaping to Vietnam their lives had been spared. Now they were back as our new rulers.

Before long the Vietnamese army requisitioned our big house by the river for their soldiers. Also the Khmer Rouge had released my uncle, and he allowed us to move in with his family. But this arrangement did not last long as the Vietnamese soon took his house, forcing us to build a little house on a vacant lot.

April 1979

To describe our new place of living as a house is misleading. If I explain how it was constructed, a better name might be found for it. It was built of wood, cloth, and tin—wood for the floor and three sides; cloth on the fourth side; and tin for the roof, that is, as far as it would go. We scavenged these articles wherever we could find them. Sleeping on our 10 by 15 foot floor made a carpet of sleepers. During rain storms there was considerable shifting as each of us tried to avoid the leaks. But it was home nonetheless. We were happy to have it, and our family was together again.

As the Kampuchean New Year came around, we had some very definite things to be thankful for and a good reason to celebrate. The Vietnamese had broken the iron rule of the Khmer Rouge, and all the known living members of our family were together again. Additionally, we had plenty of food.

Each time the Voice of America broadcast came on the air at one of our neighbors' shacks, we rushed over to hear the news. It was interesting learning about President Jimmy Carter going to both Egypt and Israel trying to bring the two nations together after years of hatred.

Every day there were more interesting news items from around the world, but the truly wonderful news, that which was most meaningful to me, was the willingness of the United States to accept Kampuchean refugees. Those tidings sent a thrill through my body every time I heard the announcer mention it.

But there was still more. The really electrifying information came when the announcer gave his name at the end of the program. It thrilled me from head to toe, for the man speaking was actually my uncle, Father's younger brother, speaking from the United States to me in Kampuchea by way of Voice of America. I knew he was telling the truth when he said that the United States would accept Kampuchean refugees. It was the same as if Uncle Eng were personally visiting with us.

Uncle Eng had been away for many years, but I had seen him often when he was living in Phnom Penh, and working for the United States Information Service. Later he had moved to the American Bangkok Program Center in Thailand before being transferred to Voice of America in Washington, D.C.

These broadcasts triggered many discussions. While

others were bickering over whether or not we should flee, my question was When do we start? I had good reasons for feeling we should leave as soon as possible. Radio reports were indicating that Pol Pot, with some of his close associates, was hiding in the mountains and preparing to drive the Vietnamese out of the country and to assume power. One of the men reported to be hiding with him was his hatchet man, Deuch, head of the Khmer Rouge's feared *Nokorbal*, the secret police. It was his sinister mind that had thought up such gruesome tortures as pouring kerosene into the vagina of young women, then setting the ladies on fire or having his men push bottles up ladies' vaginas, then smashing the bottles.

When the Vietnamese rushed through Kampuchea, they found thousands of documents listing the murders this man and his organization had committed. The documents were all hidden in S-21, which I knew as Tuol Sleng, my old high school in Phnom Penh, which had become one of the main torture centers for the Khmer Rouge. The thought of Pol Pot and his gang still in the country frightened me. I was determined to get away from them as soon as possible.

At the time, we were enjoying ample food, but the news kept indicating that a famine could be just ahead that would be worse than anything we had experienced in the past. The Khmer Rouge had helped create it by burning the rice barns and placing mines in the rice fields as they fled.

I had strong convictions on this matter, but not all of the family agreed with my enthusiasm or my reasons. Some were afraid of living and working in a Western nation. Others contended that the new government was better than the Khmer Rouge and would control the Khmer Rouge, therefore, we should stay. Their arguments did not impress me. It was true that the government had changed, but we were still under a rule that was too much like the Khmer Rouge. Kampuchea was still a red flag nation.

My sister Letine wanted to stay. Tired of running and moving, she was willing to accept the new government, at least give it a chance. *By* was for escaping, but her husband was dead set against it. Such a move would demolish his hope of ever finding his lost mother. Nakry joined me. She was thinking of the future welfare and education of her boys. My brother Sarith also wanted to leave.

As our escape group increased in size, we became bolder in our thinking and decisions. After a time those of us who wanted to leave decided on a course of action. If the others wanted to stay, that was all right with us—they had that right—but we were leaving as soon as possible.

When this new plan of action was announced, Mother stepped into the decision-making process and declared that if some of the family was going to escape, all would go. The family would stay together. She would not allow freedom to separate her loved ones if it could be avoided. Her announcement settled the issue. All of us were leaving.

Preparations started in earnest. We divided up rice into 10-day supplies for everyone and selected a few pots for cooking and a change of clothes for each one. We devised plans to get our gold, precious stones, and jewelry past the robbers that we felt we would inevitably encounter. At the last, *By*'s husband decided his family would follow along about a month later so he could complete some business.

Excitement ran high that last night, so high that few of us managed a good sleep. Tomorrow we would head for the border—and freedom. The very thought of it caused my heart to beat faster, and I managed to flood my pillow of wadded up clothes with tears of joy. Just four years and one month earlier, we had been forced to flee our home in Phnom Penh and been thrust into slavery. Now we were risking everything to regain our freedom.

Thursday, May 17, 1979

No one objected to our very early start on that special morning. Neither did the many stories of robbers roaming the countryside dampen our enthusiasm. Freedom was worth the early morning hours, even the danger of bandits.

On that same day, some 14 hours later, as the sun was

dropping beyond the trees, Mother announced that we would continue on to the next village, a short distance ahead. Moments later, as the shadows grew longer, we saw three men slowly moving out of the dark forest just ahead of us. As we approached, they held up their hands and demanded that we stop. They pointed to our oxen, accusing us of stealing them. Robbers! On our first day! No one was expecting them so soon. They were taking advantage of an unarmed family on this lonely road, and it would soon be dark.

Mother stepped forward to explain that we owned the oxen, but her explanations fell on deaf ears. Their motives were apparent. Sensing serious trouble, my brother Saat, a good-sized man at this time, began slowly moving to the front of the oxen. Stretching one arm out over each ox, he said by his actions, "You're not taking our oxen."

After standing there a few moments, he reached down and picked up a stick about two feet long and as big around as my arm. It was used to hold up the tongue of the cart when we stopped. His actions clearly indicated he was ready to use the club if the robbers attempted to take the oxen.

About the same time, Sarith started moving to the back of the cart, pulling out a long knife from under a bag of rice. He too was in a fighting mood, ready to use the knife if necessary. Tension was mounting. It was almost dark, and Nakry's little boy added to the anxiety by crying.

Hoping to avoid a fight, Mother continued talking to the men. Daylight faded as they talked, and no progress was made. Mother refused to give up the oxen, and the men kept demanding them. Saat and Sarith continued standing guard.

Finally Mother suggested that all go back to the village we had just passed and talk to the village leader. The men agreed but insisted on taking possession of the oxen before they went back. Mother refused, the boys backed her, and another long argument started. Eventually the robbers agreed we could take the oxen back. Slowly, by starlight, the boys turned the oxen and cart around.

Only the leader's wife was at home. He would not be

back until late the next day. With that news, the men demanded that the oxen be left at the leader's home. Again Mother refused. Under no circumstances was she going to allow the oxen out of our control. We would stay at the leader's home until he returned.

The boys arranged to take turns standing guard during the night. But before Mother went to sleep, one of the men came to her indicating he wanted to talk. Very bluntly he told her that in order to keep the oxen she would have to pay something. Mother responded by telling him that we lived nearby, which was true. If they knew we were traveling to the border, more would be demanded. The bargaining went back and forth for some time. Slowly his demands were lowered, and Mother ended up giving him one-eighth of an ounce of gold. Well after midnight, some 20 hours since we had left our little shack, a weary group of travelers settled down to sleep.

Friday, May 18, 1979

Three hours later Mother quietly moved among the sleepers, waking everyone up, insisting that we start immediately so as to get past the robbers' hideout before daylight. Fumbling in the darkness, the boys hitched the oxen to the cart. Then we slowly made our way through the dark village and down the same lonely road on which we had been accosted just a few hours earlier.

Saturday, May 19, 1979

"Robbers ahead! Robbers ahead!" shouted the travelers as they passed going in the opposite direction. It was time to make the final preparation for meeting them. Immediately the ladies started taking the precious stones out of the rings and jewelry, surrounding them with beeswax. I put three diamonds in the three cavities of my teeth. Additional beeswax was formed into the shape of a suppository and precious stones pushed into it. Each adult was then required to insert one beeswax suppository into his or her rectum. We sewed necklaces and bracelets into the hems of our clothes. With this matter taken care of, we bravely marched on.

The home of eleven rooms the Pheng's were driven from on April 17, 1975. Used by the Khmer Rouge for storage. Photo taken in 1990.

The temple, Wat Phnom, which legend says was built by a lady named Penh. It is supposed to have influenced the naming of the city Phnom Penh.

Vatha and the lush green rice paddies
of Cambodia.

Letine holds fruit she has not enjoyed
for years.

Vatha's old high school, Tuol Sleng which became known as S-21, the main torture center of the Khmer Rouge.

Oxen and cart similar to the one the Pheng family used as they tried to escape.

House boat on the Mekong
River. Whole families live on
these boats.

Tree used to smash the skulls of
babies and small children in the
"Killing Fields."

Guide holds human tooth at the "Killing Fields." Other teeth can be seen on the ground.

Mass grave in the "Killing Fields."

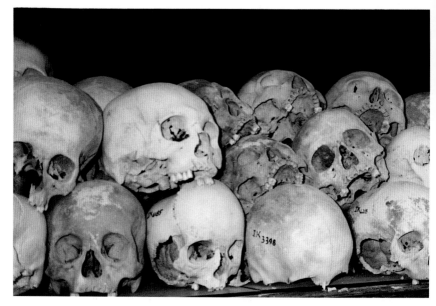

Skulls in the memorial at the "Killing Fields."

Leg bones picked up in the "Killing Fields."

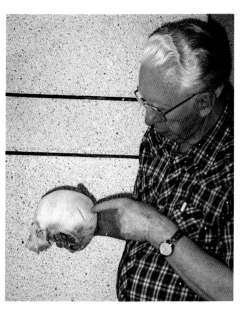

Skull found in the "Killing Fields" which apparently was hit by the blade of an ax.

Vatha viewing the pictures of prisoners tortured at S-21.

Sunrise on the Mekong River. A new
day is dawning in Cambodia.

At a small village beyond Sisophon, our anxieties changed from robbers to mine fields and the best way to get around the Vietnamese army. The guide we hired explained the route we would be following. He emphasized the danger we would be in while walking through mine fields. No one must step off the path.

Sunday, May 20, 1979

Before the first streaks of light appeared in the eastern sky, the guide lined us up. It was exciting starting out in the darkness. Freedom lay just ahead, but so were land mines, the Vietnamese Army, and more robbers. A little before the sun peeked over the eastern horizon, the guide stopped us in a dry rice field and ordered everyone to sit down. Quickly he moved from family to family, collecting the payment of three chee of gold for each person. (Eight Cambodian chee equal one ounce of gold.) With the fees all collected, the walking started again.

About mid-morning gunshots startled us. Seized with fear, our group scattered in all directions. But at gunpoint the outlaws slowly rounded us up. While two men stood guard, fingers on the triggers of their guns, others started searching for gold and precious stones. After about an hour, apparently satisfied, the raiders left.

My family managed to get by without material loss or physical injury, but the guide was gone. I'm convinced he knew that the bandits were at this place and that he would be able to get back to lead another group, collecting additional gold. We were in a strange area with no roads to follow. Fortunately, it was easy to see where others had walked. By following the trampled grass, we kept moving.

This was a rough day. Just ahead another gang was stopping and robbing every group. At the time, our family was walking with about 100 people. The first robbers of the day were Kampucheans; these were Thai. Brandishing knives, scissors, and can openers, they moved from person to person in a threatening manner. Some of our group were hiding their gold in children's diapers. All the diapers came off.

A few hours before, Leang had found an old cigarette lighter filled with gold and precious stones. Mother told him to hide it, but instead he put it in his shirt pocket. When the robbers found it, they dragged him to the center of the group and held a knife to his throat. Leang turned white with panic.

Mother was very frightened but outwardly remained calm. Using the little Thai in her vocabulary, she explained that Leang had just found the cigarette lighter a short time before. If he had been trying to hide it, he would not have put it in his shirt pocket. But they either did not understand her Kampuchean accent or did not care. They refused to release Leang. The sharp blade was almost touching his throat. All resistance among the people was completely eliminated. Everyone was terrified.

Mother continued pleading for Leang's release, and the marauders continued carefully searching each family. Suddenly, without announcement, about an hour later, Leang was released, and the bandits slowly walked into the jungle with their loot. Our only material loss was the contents of the old cigarette lighter. But the emotional damage inflicted on the family was enormous. It took considerable time for the color to return to Leang's face and even longer for us to regain our composure.

I'll never forget my aunt whom we found at a resting place. Her eyes were flashing with indignation. Robbers had found her belt containing about 13 ounces of gold. Attempting to hide it, she had wrapped it in a scarf and had put the scarf around her hair. One of the robbers grabbed the colorful scarf as he walked by, the belt with the gold going with it.

By late afternoon we had crossed the border into Thailand. The exhaustion from running, along with the nervous strain caused by the knife at Leang's throat, had drained our strength. But no amount of fatigue could dampen our enthusiasm. (See the map on next page.)

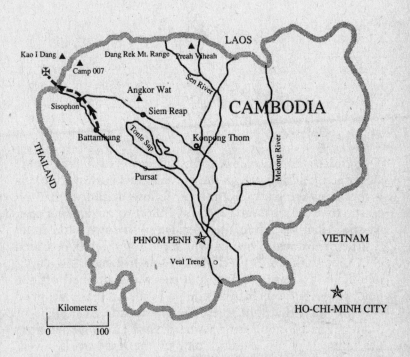

Kao I Dang ▲

Camp 007 ▲

Dang Rek Mt. Range

Preah Viheah ▲

LAOS

Sen River

Angkor Wat ▲

Sisophon ✠

CAMBODIA

Siem Reap ●

Battambang

Tonle Sap

Konpong Thom ○

Mekong River

THAILAND

Pursat

PHNOM PENH ☆

VIETNAM

Veal Treng ○

Kilometers

HO-CHI-MINH CITY ☆

0   100

May, June 1979

Hundreds of weary, excited escapees were camping in the open field just across the border. Darkness overtook us before we were ready. Rain soon followed, and we had no plastic to protect us. As water was collecting around our feet, we stood in it for a time, then decided to sit down in the mud. A little breeze was blowing, which could not really be called cold, but with our wet clothes it felt freezing. Soon after midnight the rain stopped, and the water drained off the field, so we laid our blankets down in the mud and dropped off into an exhausted sleep. This was our first night of freedom, and I didn't hear a single word of complaint from the family about the rain, cold, or the bandits. We were happy, willing to go through anything for freedom.

Thai traders surrounded us with food, pots, plastic, and other items soon after daylight the next morning. Mother was able to sell a ruby ring for 600 Thai bahts (US$30), allowing her to purchase a bucket, plastic, and a few food items.

All that day our excited family waited anxiously for an American to come and help us make our move to the United States. The sun, moving slowly across the sky, sank in the western horizon. But no American came to our camp. Another day dawned. Our hopes were high, but nothing happened. On the fourth day, a Red Cross truck appeared, but no American.

The following day, after moving a short distance to better our position, electrifying news greeted us. Buses were coming. Thai authorities were trying to unite families that had become separated. Watching these buses pull away stirred my emotions, but my courage was good. With my own ears, I had heard distinctly my uncle say that the United States was accepting Kampuchean refugees.

A beautiful Thai lady bought mother's necklace for 3,000 Thai bahts (US$150) and agreed to send a note to my uncle in the United States. A week, then two, went by. Each day we looked for an American official to help us, but none came.

Life was very primitive in the early days of the border camps. Almost all the refugees lived in makeshift shelters like ours—a few stakes driven into the ground and covered with plastic or cloth. There was no order or arrangement for the shelters. They just sprouted like weeds. With thousands of people in these cramped quarters, hygiene was difficult to maintain. In some places garbage piled up with its usual swarm of flies. Security was missing. Neither police nor soldiers were patrolling at night, leaving us without protection. This permitted stealing and the occasional rape. Most of the camps were without drinking water. At times it had to be hauled from a considerable distance. As the relief agencies became better organized, tank trucks delivered water to the different camps, and security along with hygiene improved. Why were we willing to live in these conditions without complaining? The answer is not hard to find. You would hear the same answer from almost any refugee you questioned. We were willing to endure anything to be free.

Friday, June 8, 1979

Good news ultimately arrived, sending a wave of excitement through the camp. A large number of buses were coming to the rice field where we had first camped. As we watched them pull up, our hopes soared higher than ever before. We learned that the Thai soldiers told the people that they were moving them to a better camp inside Thailand, a camp with more protection.

Hundreds of families boarded the buses. As they pulled away, we chided ourselves for having made the mistake of moving from our original camp. If only we had stayed in the rice field, we would be on a bus moving a step closer to freedom. All day we talked about it, hoping that the buses would come to our camp the next morning.

The radio announcer that evening told a shockingly different story. The large number of buses picking up hundreds of Kampuchean families were not going to freedom but were heading back to Kampuchea, back to slavery. At first I refused to believe the news, then I was sure the announcer was mixed up. But as the same story was repeated time after time that evening, I was forced to accept this terrible reality. It was true. They were going back to Kampuchea, and we would be next.

This turn of events left me speechless. Confusion reigned in the camp that night. Why? What had gone wrong? Almost every family in camp had heard the promises of freedom made by the Voice of America, promises repeated time after time. I had believed them. My family had believed them. Thousands of others had believed them. Why were they taking us back to bondage? I'll never forget Friday evening, June 8, 1979. It was one of the bleakest of my life.

Saturday, June 9, 1979

The next day was beautiful, but the alarming news of the evening before still caused tears and despair. In the early morning hours, before many of the families had finished eating their rice, my nightmares turned into realities. Buses arrived at our camp—the same kind, and it looked like the same number. Soon we heard the same story from the Thai soldiers.

They ordered us to quickly pack our things and board. But this time the reception was different. Most of the people just looked at the soldiers and refused to pack or board. We did not want that kind of protection, but the soldiers had guns, and they were determined to carry out their orders. Soon they were shooting into the air and demanding that we get on the buses. Some were pushing people and hitting them with the butt of their guns. With this show of force, the area exploded into wild confusion.

Slowly, reluctantly hundreds of betrayed, defenseless Kampuchean families, just one step from freedom, began boarding the buses. Each one knew full well that he or she was not heading to freedom, but back into servitude. To say we were sad does not describe the crushing disappointment.

As the long procession of buses started moving slowly through the countryside, hundreds of Thai people gathered by the side of the road and pushed bags of rice and water through the windows of the bus to us. This happened again several hours later when the buses stopped for fuel. It was a wonderful act of compassion. They must have known the trouble we were in and were trying to help. But we were so deeply hurt at being betrayed, it was impossible to appreciate their kindness at the time.

The buses kept traveling all morning and all afternoon. After dark our driver was forced to shift down to a lower gear. I knew we were climbing but had no idea where. About midnight, some 14 hours later, the buses stopped, unloaded us, then disappeared into the darkness. We were abandoned in a wilderness. In the moonlight I could see nothing but trees and bushes all around. Our family huddled close together. After talking a few minutes, an exhausted and hopelessly confused refugee family stretched out their mats on the rocky ground and sought sleep. (See the map on next page.)

Sunday, June 10, 1979
The next morning, as color began appearing in the eastern sky, scores of people were up, hoping to see the road into Kampuchea, but they were disappointed. It was still too dark to see anything but blackness in that direction, but sunlight soon displaced the darkness, revealing a horrifying view.

Behind us soldiers were guarding the road leading to

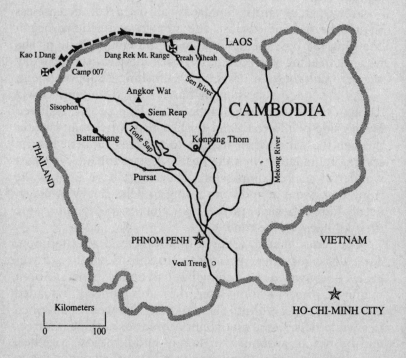

Kao I Dang

Camp 007

Dang Rek Mt. Range   Preah Viheah   LAOS

Sen River

Sisophon

Angkor Wat

Siem Reap

CAMBODIA

THAILAND

Battambang

Tonle Sap

Konpong Thom

Mekong River

Pursat

PHNOM PENH

Veal Treng

VIETNAM

Kilometers

0   100

HO-CHI-MINH CITY

freedom. In the other direction, toward Kampuchea, the terrain dropped down at a very steep angle. It looked almost straight down. We were on the edge of a cliff. There were no roads and not even a path or a place to make one. I saw nothing but large boulders, trees, and heavy underbrush. Getting over this cliff and down the mountain looked impossible.

The range of mountains we were on divides Kampuchea and Thailand. I knew of this mountain range from my study, but had never been in the area before. The gradual approach on the Thai side, along with the precipitous drop on the Kampuchean side, matched my knowledge of the area. If I remembered my lessons correctly, we were in an isolated part of the country—far from people and food.

Many of the refugees who had arrived the day before were still on the mountain, confused and afraid. Some could not move. This included a poor old lady barely able to walk. I found her sitting on the ground, leaning up against a tree. Her face was buried in her hands. She looked completely dejected. Her daughter had managed to get her to Thailand by hiring men to carry her, but it was impossible to hire anyone at this place to carry her nor could she go back. As a result, the daughter had been forced to leave her mother behind, alone on the mountaintop and facing death as soon as her little supply of rice and water was exhausted.

Checking our supply of water indicated that we had very little for our group. Our two containers, holding a total of two and a half gallons, would have to be rationed among 10 people, for no one knew when more water would be found.

Slowly families near us started working their way over the cliff. We followed. Each adult carried a bundle, and the men assisted or carried the children. The strongest went first to help break the fall if someone lost his or her footing. With no path to follow, we moved down as best we could. At times we slid down big boulders while we clung to vines for support. At other times, we handed the children to someone below us.

105

By the middle of the hot afternoon, we had covered about 100 yards.

Beads of perspiration glistened on every face. Each one was craving water, but our thirst could not be satisfied nor did we want to use water to cook rice. Our dire situation was hard enough for the adults to handle, but impossible for the children to understand. In desperation, some men went from family to family, offering gold for a little water. Very few accepted the offer.

Monday, June 11, 1979

About noon the second day some of the first families, who had begun climbing down the mountain the day before we arrived, reached the valley. With no one ahead of them, they could move faster. With the mountainside crowded with people, much of our time was spent in waiting for the families ahead to move before we could advance. Those reaching the floor of the valley started the search for water. Shortly after, a shout came up from below that we could hear on the mountainside. Someone had found water.

By this time, many families were desperately thirsty. At the news of water, men, who could move faster, began rushing down the mountain, leaving the women and children behind. Our family still had a little water so the boys did not go. We continued to work our way slowly down.

A short time after the glorious shout of water, another sound came rolling up the mountainside—the terrifying sound of explosions. Hardly a person moved. No one knew what caused the explosions, but we all knew that something was terribly wrong. Obviously death lay just ahead. In a matter of minutes, news of land mines around the water came up the mountain almost as fast as the sound of the explosions. Some men had been killed.

Many hours later those men who had rushed down for water started returning. They looked weary, but their families were happy to see them because their men were out of danger and had water. The youngsters were jumping with joy.

While some were celebrating, others were weeping. Nearby a widow with several small children was completely out of water. She was desperate. Crying, the young lady went from family to family begging a few drops. Unfortunately, the human desire for survival was so strong that only a few families were willing to share with her. Hours went by, more men failed to return from the valley, and as families began realizing their loss, tears flowed.

Tuesday, June 12, 1979

With land mines in the valley below, the people started seriously deliberating about returning to the top of the mountain. Maybe the Thai soldiers would help them find a safe path. It seemed there was nothing but death below. As this thought spread, more and more agreed with the idea. Finally everyone stopped going down. For a few minutes the lines stood still. Then slowly we turned around, starting the almost impossible task of retracing our steps.

In a matter of minutes my legs were ready to buckle. Weak to begin with, I found it almost impossible to make the ascent. The rocks seemed two and three times larger than they actually were. Those we had slid down, we now had to climb or find a way around. Going down was easy compared to going up.

Not long after we had turned around, we heard gunshots at the top of the mountain. Again we froze in our tracks. More trouble. The news soon came down. Thai soldiers had killed several people and were standing with rifles pointing at us. They would kill anyone who did not turn around and go down the mountain. It was a desperate situation—land mines at the bottom and Thai soldiers with pointed rifles at the top. No matter which way we went, death faced us. We were trapped on this rugged mountainside, had not eaten for three days, and our supply of water was almost exhausted.

Darkness was falling fast, adding to the confusion and dilemma. Not knowing what to do, we did nothing. Our family drew as close together as possible. The descent was so steep that sleeping space was at a premium, and some of the family slept sitting up, leaning against a rock or tree, so the children could stretch out for a good rest. During the night it rained, but it was impossible to catch any for drinking.

At sunrise, I learned about a young mother, not far from our position, who had given birth to a baby during those dark rainy hours. It was a miserable night for me, but I could not complain after hearing about the young lady with the new baby. A Kampuchean would say she had *Chhlang Tonle*, which means "crossed the river." Kampucheans had crossed many rivers. It was dangerous, and some people drowned. Childbirth was like crossing one of Kampuchea's rivers. It was dangerous, for it could cause death.

Wednesday, June 13, 1979

After a night's sleep and more discussion, we decided that we should continue climbing down the mountain, hoping we might find a path through the mine fields.

The next night was also terrible. Rain would have been welcome. At least it would have moistened our lips, and it might have been possible to catch some in our plastic. My little nephew, Visal, suffered so from thirst. He would fall asleep, then in a few minutes wake up crying and begging for water. I was so deeply hurt over his suffering that I forgot my own desperate thirst. Four spoonfuls was all he could have. He wanted more, but the rest had to be saved. There was just enough for each one to have about four spoonfuls of water the next morning. Then the containers would be empty.

Thursday, June 14, 1979

With the last of our water gone, two of the boys volunteered to go down the mountain for more. They knew the danger and promised to exercise extreme caution. We could not go on. With nothing to eat and only spoonfuls of water to drink for several days, our strength was about gone. Some in our group, myself included, could barely stand up.

I hated to see the boys go into the mine fields. Both were younger than I—Saat 19, Lim only 15. Other men had gone down and died. Tearfully we agreed to stay in the same place.

After they left, the hours dragged on as though they were days. With time seeming almost to stand still, our imaginations were working overtime. We could not avoid conjecturing about the terrible possibility of the boys not returning. We were desperate. If they did not return with water, most of us would not have the strength to continue.

More than seven hours passed before we spotted the boys slowly climbing back up to our precarious position on the mountain. Our strained faces relaxed. Smiles, stained with tears, broke out on our faces. Their containers were full of water, dirty water, but it was water, and no one was limited to four spoonfuls. After allowing us to drink all the water we wanted, they surprised us by opening a pan of cooked rice. .Without any of the family realizing it, the boys had taken rice and a pan with them. After getting water, they had gathered some wood, cooked the rice, and had eaten some.

How thoughtful of them! We did not have to gather wood, build a fire, and wait for the rice to cook. It was a feast of plain, cold, unsalted rice on the side of a steep mountain—the first meal we'd had in several days. Our situation was still serious, but with water, rice, and the safe return of the boys, we had hope.

While we ate that special meal, the boys told us about conditions near the water. After walking a short distance in the valley, they had spotted the water. As they approached it, they walked one behind the other, stepping in the other's footsteps. Bodies were strewn all around them. They told how it had been necessary to step carefully over some of the corpses before they could reach the water. Their story frightened me. We were very fortunate to have them back. After we had eaten our meal, we had no difficulty descending to the valley.

Walking again on near level ground, we speculated as to how many people had been forced back into Kampuchea during June 8, 9, and 10. We learned that my brother Lim had counted the buses on the first two days—40 each day. He also had counted the number of people on our bus—80.

Assuming the Thai government was using the same fleet of buses on the next day, the 10th, it would mean that more than 3,000 people each day had been deported, making a total of between 9,000 and 10,000 men, women, and children. I have heard about other large groups of Kampucheans being pushed back but have no personal information about them. However, the Issue Paper of the U.S. Committee for Refugees claims that more than 44,000 Kampucheans were pushed back between June 8-12.

It says they were pushed "back into Cambodia through a mountainous border region" and "forced at gunpoint over the precipice." "Those who panicked at the edge and tried to run back were shot." Thousands "died, many from the fall, and others as they tried to cross the mine field at the bottom of the cliff" ("People on the Edge," U.S. Committee for Refugees, Issue Paper, Cambodians in Thailand, Dec. 1985, p. 10).

Why did the government of Thailand decide to force some 44,000 helpless Kampucheans back into a life of slavery? The U.S. Committee for Refugees gives the following answer. "Faced with the possibility that nearly one-half million Cambodians might cross the Thai border in 1979, Bangkok worried about the international community's apparent ambivalence in responding to Thai security needs. As the numbers grew beyond Thailand's perceived ability to protect its borders, Bangkok searched for a powerful symbolic response illustrating its determination to maintain control. Finally, that summer, Bangkok announced the forced repatriation of Cambodians within Thailand, saying they created an intolerable security threat to the country" (*ibid.*).

June 1979

Physically we had escaped from the danger of the cliffs, but it still haunted our thinking. My aunt, father's sister—the one who was so willing to help us with rice and medicine when we needed it—was not well when she had started for the Thai border. The entire trip had been extremely hard on her, but getting down the mountain was too much. She almost reached the valley, but that was all. We had to leave her body in a shallow grave near a rock. Her bones, along with those of many others, will be a perpetual reminder of the sorrow, suffering, and death experienced by people seeking to regain their freedom but were pushed back and abandoned on a mountain range called Dang Rek.

It was a relief to reach the valley, but our problems were not over. Water was available, but our supply of rice was very low. Also, we were in a heavily wooded area, with no idea of how many miles there might be between us and inhabitants. Most disturbing was the danger of stepping on land mines.

Ahead of us many families were stopping at the edge of the mine field, afraid to go on. Already a number had been killed trying to cross it. But going back was impossible. Our rice was almost gone, so there was nothing to do but join the single line that was slowly winding its way to the other side. Each person was stepping in the footsteps of the one ahead. Adults were either carrying their children or forcing them to walk directly in front of them.

The mined area was less than a quarter mile long, but the path that snaked through it was much longer. The single line of humanity moved very slowly. Darkness was approaching as we reached the other side, which forced us to camp for the night.

Safely past the mine field and having had a good night's sleep, we were ready to face a new day of walking. Just after noon, word reached us about a Vietnamese Army headquarters about five miles ahead, where food was available. This was good news, for we had used up all our rice. Joining the long line near one of the hut-like military buildings, we slowly worked our way to the door. When we went inside, our hopes were dashed. No rice was available, but they did give us a little flour and salt.

Each one of our group was weak from lack of food and water during the past few days. In addition many were suffering from sore legs and swollen feet. The children were very irritable, and some were sick. But we must keep moving. Each day the ordeal of walking started soon after daylight and continued until just before dark. As the days passed, colds, diarrhea, and fever were added to our list of discomforts, but every day we kept on walking.

Reaching the Sen River helped boost our sagging courage. There, a camp of Vietnamese soldiers guarded the river crossing. In order to cross, we had to obtain permission from an army officer. While making arrangements for this crossing, *By*'s husband was arrested. The charge: "Assisting Chinese people across the river." My skin is quite light, and Sokhom has darker skin. They took him to be Kampuchean, and considered us Chinese, who were not allowed to cross.

When the Vietnamese occupied Kampuchea, they made it difficult for the Chinese. Politics was behind the way the Vietnamese treated the Chinese. Vietnam was backed by Russia. China was backing the Khmer Rouge. Furthermore, relations between Russia and China were not the best. This made trouble for the Chinese refugees who wanted to cross the river, and it was a serious matter for us. We had lost all our documents for identification when we fled our home in Phnom Penh. If we could not establish our Cambodian nationality, the Vietnamese soldiers would not permit us to cross the river.

Mother talked to the officers, but it did no good. We were desperate, without documents and without food. Day after day the boys went into the woods to dig bamboo shoots. The taste was terrible—sharp and bitter—but they did help keep us alive, for there was nothing else to eat.

On the fourth day, *By* and I met a Vietnamese officer. She spoke to him in English, and he understood. This gave us a chance to explain that we were not Chinese but Kampucheans and that Sokhom was just helping his own family. The officer asked a few questions, then wrote a letter granting us permission to cross. With this letter in hand, things moved quickly. On the other side of the river, rice was available, and our family was permitted to ride on a truck that was returning empty, saving a few miles of walking.

At one of the checkpoints, the army required us to sign our names, indicating whether we wanted to go to Phnom Penh or Battambang. We enthusiastically added our names to the Battambang list, thinking it meant a truck ride to our destination. But there was a catch. This special transportation was only for the sick, old, or pregnant, which allowed mother, Nakry, and her boy who had measles, and *By*, who was pregnant, to ride on a truck. How *By*'s husband managed to get on, I never found out. For he was neither sick, old, nor pregnant. The rest of us had to walk.

Several days later we were shocked to see mother with the others waiting for us at the side of the road. The truck had taken them about 44 miles before putting them off, so they had camped while waiting for us. In a few days, they were again allowed to ride, arriving in Battambang several days ahead of us. It was about the middle of July when we walked into the city.

For more than two weeks we had camped on the border of freedom, but had been rejected. Now the long walk of almost one month was over. It had started near the old temple ruins of Preah Vihear. From the mountaintop, where we were left by the buses, to Battambang was about 280 miles. (See the map on next page.)

July 1979
Slowly the process of reestablishing ourselves moved forward. Food was hard to secure because we lacked gold. Consequently, when we heard about securing gold by smuggling we were interested. Saat and Sokhom were the first to go to Thailand and bring back merchandise to sell in Kampuchea. It worked, and Saat brought back some gold, enabling us to have extra rice.

Lim and Nakry also tried it. Lim earned 1,000 Thai bahts (US$50) before a Thai soldier forced him to give up all his money, and then returned 100 bahts (US$5). But it took more than this to discourage Lim. The two kept working

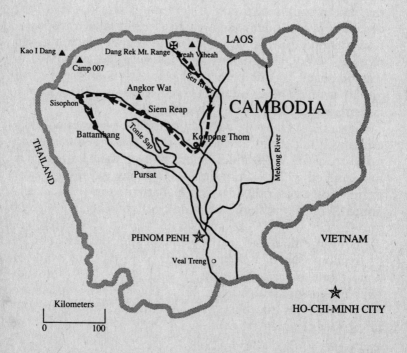

until they were able to buy more merchandise.

Leaving Thailand, they stopped to sleep at a *samnak* where others were spending the night. Sometime before morning, a Thai soldier tossed a grenade near the sleeping people, not near enough to injure them but close enough to scare them away so he could get their merchandise. Lim ran and Nakry also ran, but not before picking up her goods.

Smuggling became a necessity for our survival. Several members of the family were either at the Thai border or traveling back and forth most of the time, making a round trip of about 125 miles. After several months, the family moved to the border, where we could trade and earn enough money for rice, eliminating the risk of meeting soldiers and robbers or losing our lives or merchandise in high water. Plus, we would be closer to freedom. *By* waited till after the baby was born to make her trip to the border. The new arrival was a sweet little black-haired girl whom *By* called Anname. The date: Friday, September 14, 1979.

Early October 1979

When *By* was stronger and able to make the move to the border, the first part of the trip was uneventful. Near Thailand they spotted a Vietnamese soldier inspecting everyone who came along. *By*, her baby, and Annong, along with Letine and Leang, were riding on a cart pulled by a horse. Sarith, carrying a piece of silver in the shape of a tomato, was riding *By*'s bicycle.

The sight of the Vietnamese soldier caused Sarith to remember the silver he was carrying. He was determined to get it through safely, so he started pedaling at full speed. He, along with the horse and cart, arrived at the soldier's post of duty at the same time. The soldier was standing in the middle of the road, frantically waving his arms in an attempt to stop Sarith. But he whizzed by without slackening his speed.

Shocked at Sarith's disregard of his authority, the soldier sprang into action, firing a shot into the air, then jumping on his bicycle. Instead of the shot stopping Sarith, it frightened the horse, causing him to leap into the air. The sudden jerk on the cart threw Letine off headfirst onto the road. *By* picked her up and helped her back onto the cart. A quick examination showed a bruise or two on her head, and she was dazed for a few moments but otherwise not seriously hurt.

Meanwhile the soldier was racing down the road, trying to catch Sarith, who was well ahead and showing no signs of stopping. The soldier fired another shot. This one caused Sarith to have second thoughts about outrunning a soldier. Carrying the silver tomato through safely did not seem worth getting a bullet in his back. When the soldier caught up to Sarith, he checked the baggage, missing the silver tomato, and allowed Sarith to continue on.

Smugglers, heading for Kampuchea, warned *By* of more soldiers just ahead. This made it necessary to stop near a village and hide until dark. Moving again, off the road in the darkness and rain, *By* and Letine became separated. At this time Letine's weight was less than 60 pounds. Yet she managed to carry *By*'s two-year-old girl, Annong, most of the way when they were off the main road. Moving slowly along in the darkness, Letine heard the sound of carts coming behind her. Immediately she hurried off the path, pushing herself with Annong up against a tree. It was just in time, for one water buffalo after another, each pulling a cart filled with people and belongings, went by in the darkness less than three feet from them.

Disregarding the need to make as little noise as possible, every few minutes *By* would call to see if Letine and the boys were coming along. Fortunately, she overtook an old man, his wife, and son. The old lady told *By* to be quiet, slow down, and follow them. She obeyed, allowing Letine and the boys to catch up gradually. Before long they reached the border. (See the map on next page.)

Late October 1979

A former commander in the Cambodian army asked Sokhom to join his border resistance camp, where many of the soldiers Sokhom had served with were living. Our whole

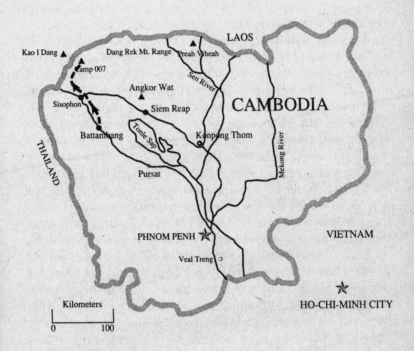

LAOS

Kao I Dang ▲

Dang Rek Mt. Range   Preah Viheah ▲

Camp 007

Sen River

Angkor Wat ▲

Sisophon

Siem Reap

CAMBODIA

Battambang

Tonle Sap

Konpong Thom

Mekong River

Pursat

THAILAND

PHNOM PENH ☆

VIETNAM

Veal Treng

Kilometers

0   100

HO-CHI-MINH CITY ☆

family moved with him, for mother was still trying very hard to keep the family together.

Soon after our arrival in the military camp, a group of journalists were observed interviewing the camp commander. Among them Sokhom spotted a man who looked strangely like Nakry's dead husband. He quickly reported the strange sighting to the family. Returning with him to get a closer look at the familiar-looking stranger, I was shocked and amazed. Sokhom was right. Just looking at the man gave me an eerie feeling, something like looking at a person who was dead and had just come back to life. Upon investigation, we learned that he was not a journalist, but in fact a Cambodian who had joined the group so he could look for his relatives. There was a good reason for his looking like Nakry's husband. He was his younger brother.

Ten years earlier Father had helped him flee Cambodia for France. Now he was back, searching for his family. He told us to list all the names of our family, promising to send them to my uncle in the United States. Then he was gone. Everything happened so fast it was like a dream.

Two weeks later a string of explosions startled us. Rockets were coming from the Thai army. Scooping up children, babies, and our few supplies, we ran to the other side of a hill, hiding behind trees, in ditches, a few of us just lying flat on the ground. Almost two hours passed while we remained frozen in our positions.

Suddenly our protection was penetrated by a lone rocket. Fearful that others might be following, we ran again. This time we fled to the protected sandbag area of the camp military headquarters. Just as we arrived, a rocket exploded nearby, sending a splinter into Letine's arm. In confusion we ran for the path that led through the woods to Camp 204. After an hour of slow running and fast walking we stopped, completely exhausted. We could still hear the sound of exploding rockets in the distance, but we were safe and Letine's arm was not seriously hurt.

The border was quiet for another 10 days before more

rockets came our way. This time it was the Vietnamese Army who were the aggressors, causing us to make another mad scramble to the woods. The attack did not last long, and as soon as it was over Red Cross trucks picked up the wounded.

November 1979

While we camped near the border, our thoughts concentrated more and more on freedom. We wanted to get into one of the Thai refugee camps. This possibility again caused serious discussions. Most of us wanted to go, but Sokhom had not found his mother and was afraid he would never see her again if he left Kampuchea. Not wanting to divide the family, we waited several days while he wrestled with the consequences of such a move. Finally he decided to go, and this caused things to move quickly. In a matter of minutes, we broke camp up and were walking toward the border, which was about 30 minutes away. On the other side, we received a little medicine and learned there would be no more trucks going to the refugee camp before the next day.

Before daylight the next morning, our camp was alive with activity. Fires dispelled the darkness as hundreds of families cooked rice. It was an exciting time. Everyone was ready to go, but nothing happened that morning. Shortly before noon, a roar went up from the camp—the trucks were coming. Thai soldiers filled the trucks so full it was almost impossible to move. But despite the crowded conditions, Thursday, November 22, 1979, was a glorious day for me. We were heading for a new camp, Khao I Dang, administered by the United Nations High Commission for Refugees. (See the map on next page.)

Adjusting to the new freedom found in the camp was hard at first. The staff were so kind I found it necessary to pinch myself to make sure it was not all just a dream. Many times I had dreamed of reaching a refugee camp only to wake up in a slave camp, but this time it was a joyous reality.

Our first official act was to register our names and camp address on the United States Tracing Card posted near the headquarters. Next we sent a message to my uncle in Washington, D.C. Then we waited and waited while the paperwork slowly moved through the offices of the United States government. Checking the United States bulletin board for our names three or four times a day became a regular routine.

Soon after arriving in camp, my English was put to work translating for a Swedish medical team. For the first time in more than four years, working was a pleasure. When the

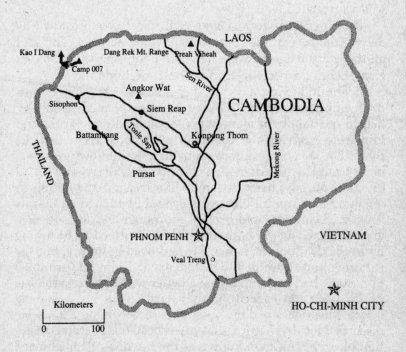

Swedish team opened a new hospital, I moved to the new pediatric ward. The three months of training that they gave the refugee nurse-girls was very helpful. Working between the doctors was hard, because of the long hours, but very enjoyable. For the first time in more than four years my work was appreciated.

By's husband worked with a medical group known as SAWS (the Seventh-day Adventist Welfare Service). This and all the other religions were new and confusing to me, for in Kampuchea 95 percent of the people are Buddhist.

In the following days, we became well acquainted with the members of the Seventh-day Adventist Church, and they helped our family in many ways. Soon Sokhom, Sarith, and Lim were studying the Christian guidebook known as the Bible. The idea of my family studying this unknown religious book troubled me. After all, we were Cambodians, and for all practical purpose being a Cambodian meant being Buddhist.

Buddhism was all I knew. In school I had learned that its founder, Gautama, had been a good man and the son of a great king. Gautama himself had been destined to be a king upon the death of his father. He had lived in luxury, but the suffering and death of the people around him had troubled him, so he had decided to seek a better way of life. At the age of 29, Gautama rode from his palace on his horse, having rejected his riches and the possibility of becoming a king. He discarded his royal attire, shaved his head, and became a very humble, religious man known as the Buddha or Enlightened One. His life and teachings have inspired others to follow his example, and it continues today as millions follow the teachings of Buddhism.

Occasionally Mother would invite the Buddhist bonzes to our home. During the rituals that they performed, we were required to sit on the floor in silence, giving close attention even though we could not understand the strange language they used. While the bonzes would go through their liturgies, we would bow several times. In this act we were always on our knees, hands on the floor with our heads touching our hands. The religious rites completed, the bonzes blessed both the house and family, this time in our national language. I didn't really understand all of the Buddhist religion, nor am I sure I believed it, but still I considered myself a loyal Buddhist.

Before long some of the family were talking about being baptized here in the camp. Letine and I were also invited to study their guidebook, be baptized, and join the church, but we declined. Working with the medical team was all that interested me.

Soon Sarith, Lim, and Sokhom became Christians, which presented an opportunity for me to learn more about the curious ceremony called baptism. Standing where I could observe all that took place, I actually watched an Adventist monk (they call them "ministers") take people down into a pond of water. Then he shocked me by pushing their heads completely under the water. Since I have a fear of water, this kind of activity frightened me. But those who were baptized said that the Bible taught this, and they seemed happy in their new religion.

March 1980

The horrors of the past were behind us, and we were looking forward to the future with great joy. But a chance meeting occurred that resurrected the sorrows and hurts of the Khmer Rouge days. While Mother was walking through the hospital grounds, she suddenly came face to face with the man who was responsible for Father's death. For a long moment the two stared at each other in complete silence. Then he suddenly turned and hurried away. Not a word passed between them, but volumes were shooting back and forth in their eyes.

When Mother arrived back at our little shack and told the family about seeing this hated man, two of the boys were ready to hunt him down and settle the score. I don't know what they intended to do, but it was clear that they were angry. In fact, all of us felt that it was unfair for such a killer to enjoy the hospitality of the democratic nations.

Back in January 1979 when the Vietnamese had broken

the power of the Khmer Rouge, many Kampucheans who had been tortured and forced to work as slaves, turned on their taskmasters, killing many of them. For the boys to have feelings of revenge was hardly surprising.

In spite of all the suffering the village leader had brought upon our family, Mother did not believe in the kind of revenge the boys seemed to have in mind. It was difficult, but she eventually succeeded in quieting them by explaining that if they did any harm to the former leader, they, too, would be guilty of the same kind of crimes he had perpetrated. The question came up, what kind of revenge was Father talking about when he said, "Tell my children to get revenge for me."

July 1980

Walking through the camp on July 12, I glanced at the United States bulletin board, as I had done hundreds of times during the past eight months. For a moment, I thought I was having a delusion, for there on the board was my name. It was impossible to run fast enough to give the news to the others. Together we started jumping up and down and shouting, "We're free! We're free!" Tears ran down my cheeks as I laughed and cried. It was the news we had been dreaming about for years.

September 1980

The required picture of our family was in our possession, my uncle had agreed to sponsor us, and we were eager for action. It finally came after we moved to another refugee camp, Chon Buri. Very formally, a United States Immigration Officer required us to stand, raise our right hands and swear to tell the truth. With this ceremony over, the first question was addressed to me. "Do you have a sister in France?" I said Yes, for Nakry had been gone about two months.

Without another word the officer reached across his desk, picked up a big rubber stamp, inked it, and stamped a word across the back of our picture. Looking at me he said, "Case closed." Then standing up he motioned toward the door, indicating that we should leave. Something was wrong, dreadfully wrong, but I had no idea what the man was talking about when he said, "Case closed" or why he was so hasty in ushering us out of his office. I was afraid to ask, and no one explained.

Outside I kept looking at those big black letters stamped on the back of our picture. It was a word I had never seen before. *REJECTED*. What did it mean? My limited knowledge of English was of no help, but from the way the man was acting, I knew that something was seriously wrong. Others who were accepted had a stamp on their hand. What did this stamp on our picture mean? A confused family hurried to our shelter, picked up the English-Cambodian dictionary, and searched for that new word, *REJECTED*.

When the definition was finally spotted, I was horrified— just about speechless. I could not believe the dictionary. Again and again I read the definition, checking to make sure I was looking at the right word. There was no doubt about it. *REJECTED* meant "turned down, refused." Our worst fears were becoming a reality. It was happening again. The United States was refusing to accept us.

Questions, anger, and tears all became mixed together during the next few hours. Why, after five years of suffering, with our goal so close to being realized, would the United States reject us? We had a sponsor. As far as I knew everything was in order, but there it was on our picture in big black letters *REJECTED*.

Before it was possible for us to see the immigration officer again, many families left for the United States. Time after time, with tears—and I must admit some resentment—we watched them go, not understanding why they could go, but we were *REJECTED*.

A ray of hope broke through the dark clouds when my aunt suddenly appeared from the United States. She is Thai, having married Father's brother, who worked for Voice of America in Washington, D.C. Her help with the United States Embassy and the money she gave us was a real boost. But her greatest and most valuable gift was the hope she brought to a very discouraged family. As she left, we felt sure of working out our problem and sooner or later gaining our freedom.

In my next visit with the immigration officer, he explained that our closest relative was my sister Nakry. So, according to him, it was the responsibility of France to take us. He was surprised to learn that Nakry had been in France just a few months and was unable to sponsor us. The officer gave us a solution. We must send a letter to Nakry explaining the mix-up. She must send a letter back indicating that she was unable to sponsor us. Then her letter must be submitted to the United States Embassy in Bangkok. Obviously it involved a long delay, but now our hopes were really high again.

The letter was rushed off. Days, weeks, months of delay followed. Her letter eventually arrived, and we gave it to the immigration officer. More delay followed, but the long-hoped-for day came eventually when our names were posted again on the United States bulletin board.

The immigration officer who had stamped that ugly black word *REJECTED* across the back of our picture now informed us we had two sponsors. *By*'s doctor friend had included us along with *By*'s family in a sponsorship to Hawaii, and my uncle was sponsoring us to Maryland. The officer asked, "Where do you folks want to go, Maryland or Hawaii?" Our hearts were set on being with my uncle so I told him, Maryland. He replied with just one word, "Idiot!" Another new and strange English word. Again, I had to go to my dictionary. The definition didn't sound very flattering, but now things were moving again.

The purpose of the next camp we moved to was to prepare us for entering the United States. For two weeks they instructed us in practical things such as how to use flush toilets, where to apply for welfare benefits, how to apply for a Social Security card, what to do if a wallet were lost or stolen, how to light a gas oven, how to go shopping in an American store, and on and on. It was a busy and interesting time.

Next we moved to Lumphini for a short 24-hour stop. Just enough time for the last medical tests. At 9:00 that evening we were at the Bangkok airport, where we received our official travel documents, which served as our passports. With these precious keys to freedom in our hands, we waited for the plane. It was an exciting time. So close to our goal. Under the circumstances sleep was impossible. Midnight came, then 3:00 a.m., but no plane arrived. As the hours dragged on, it was difficult to keep our imaginations from putting the worst construction on the delay. We had been rejected twice. Was it happening again? Slowly excitement gave way to anxiety. Almost every eye was glued on the big clock with the hands that moved ever so slowly toward morning. At last at 5 a.m., an emotionally drained family boarded the TransAmerica jet headed for the land of freedom.

Once in that giant plane, the largest I had ever been on, I was sure all my problems were over. But the plane was no more than well off the ground when I began experiencing funny feelings in my stomach. Soon my head was spinning. Then foul-smelling stuff started coming up. Fortunately, the ordeal didn't last long. Despite the sick feeling in my stomach, I was still one very happy girl.

March 1981

Two short refueling stops, and we were home—our new home, the United States of America. As we came in for a landing at Oakland, California, the flight attendant announced that it was 9:07 a.m., Pacific Standard Time, Tuesday, March 24, 1981. It was good to know the time and the day of the week again. Ten time zones and the date line had us badly mixed up. Oakland Airport looked like most other airports I had seen, but there was one big difference. This was the United States, the home of the people who were graciously opening their arms to a homeless family, allowing us to start life over again.

Many times in the past I had seen the picture of the Statue of Liberty. Although I knew very little about the United

States, every time I saw that lady holding the torch of freedom high, it excited me. There was no Statue of Liberty at Oakland Airport nor any beautiful words of invitation like those found at the base of the statue—"Give me your tired, your poor, Your huddled masses yearning to breathe free . . ."—but when the big jet rolled to a stop the electrifying thrill that surged through my body was no less than that which hundreds of thousands of others had experienced in New York at Ellis Island.

Actually, my joy may have been greater than theirs. For those refugees had to go through all kinds of examinations after they arrived, and those who didn't pass were deported. Some of the rejected were unable to bear the thought of returning to their homeland so chose to end their life by jumping into the water that surrounds Ellis Island.

I understood their desperation. Twice I was rejected. No one can really comprehend the depth of discouragement a person experiences at such a time, unless he or she has been through the same disappointment. Only then can it truly be understood. It can't be described. It's too deep, too wrenching.

The flight from Bangkok to Oakland took 18 and 1/2 hours. We were tired, airsick, but mighty happy as we staggered off the plane. For the past few weeks filling out papers for the officials in the refugee camps had been an everyday affair. Oakland was no exception. But with the immigration people satisfied, we stepped outside where officials were calling Cambodian names, helping refugees find their waiting sponsors.

Buses soon arrived for the trip across the Bay Bridge to San Francisco. Courteous young ladies helped us find our hotel rooms. At this point, the culture shock set in. The room was clean, no bugs. I had not slept in a bed like this since we were driven from our home. For six years my only bed had been a mat either on the ground or on boards, my only pillow, a wad of clothes.

While I was getting acquainted with our room, a young

lady knocked at the door and informed us it was time to eat. Since most of us were still airsick, food was the last thing any of us wanted, but no one would miss the first meal in the United States. It was wonderful, and we ate all we wanted. Mixed with the rice was something green that was new to us, small pieces of iceberg lettuce. After dinner each of us received a coat and warm socks. They were welcome, for March in the United States is much colder than March in Kampuchea.

Seven o'clock the next morning found us heading for the San Francisco Airport, then Washington, D.C. Seven hours later we touched down at National Airport. Friends and relatives met the two other Cambodian families traveling with us, but no one was there whom we recognized. We were in the United States, knew my uncle worked for Voice of America in Washington, D.C., and lived in a place called Silver Spring, Maryland, but that was all. Feelings of panic began gripping me. Crowds of people milled all around us, but we were afraid to speak to them. I saw a telephone, but had no idea how to work it or how to look up my uncle's name in the phone book. After we waited a long time, he walked up to my mother. Wonderful feelings surged through me when I arrived at his home. It was a feeling of complete security that took hold, something I had not experienced since being in my own home with my parents in Phnom Penh.

April, May 1981

March slipped into April and April into May as my uncle helped us through a ream of paper work, medical exams, applications for Social Security cards, and so on. With these details out of the way, he started looking for an apartment for us. Every phone call seemed to go the same. The apartment manager would ask how many were in the family. My uncle answered six. Then the manager would say, "Sorry, we do not allow more than four people in a three-bedroom apartment. Thank you for calling. Goodbye." Finally, in desperation, my uncle rented an apartment for his own family of four, moved out, and allowed us to live in his home.

CHAPTER

A drastic change has taken place in my life since I came to the United States. Looking back over the past few years, I can see significant changes in my objectives. Most of that time was preoccupied with survival. The next meaningful drive was escape. In my new country, much of my time at first was spent in getting a good education, providing for my family, and getting into a line of service that would enable me to help others less fortunate than I.

My attitude toward religion has also changed. In Cambodia and in the border camps, religion meant nothing to me. But after arriving in the United States, I became interested in spiritual things. Recently I have become a Christian, joining the same denomination my brothers had joined when we were in Thailand.

This shift in attitude came about in a rather unusual way. Three months after arriving in the States a man stopped by our home and introduced himself as a volunteer who was helping Cambodian refugees. He needed help, for many of the people he was assisting could not speak a word of English and he could not speak Cambodian. Would Letine and I serve as his translators?

We agreed. It was fun working with him. Not only were we aiding people from our own country, but we were also learning new English words as he helped the new arrivals obtain mattresses, get medical examinations, fill out applications for Social Security cards, enroll the children in school, and engage in the many other tasks that are overwhelming to refugees who cannot speak English.

Before long this man asked us if we would be willing to translate for him at some meetings he was going to hold with the refugees. Even though I was a Buddhist, I soon found myself translating stories from the Bible as our American friend told them, first in the living room of one of the Cambodian families then in the home of his daughter so he could accommodate the large number who were attending. This went on for more than a year. During this time, I was not only expanding my English vocabulary but was also encountering many interesting things from the Bible, including reasons for hope in Jesus Christ, which had never come to my attention before. Then I received another request. Would I translate as the American taught the Bible to several different families in their homes. Once again I agreed, and my knowledge of the Bible increased even more. Since that time, it's been my privilege to take Bible lessons from our American friend. He baptized me in June of 1986.

My past had been filled with a religion that was void of hope when compared to Christianity, and it was based on a do-it-yourself concept. I have now learned that Christ forgives my sins when I seek forgiveness and that He gives me power to overcome sin in my life when I commit myself to Him in faith. The Bible says it better than I can. "I can do all things through Christ which strengtheneth me" (Philippians 4:13). Christ is the One who gives me the strength and the power.

The traditional Cambodian dance known as *Apsara* portrays the myth of the beautiful young lady whom the gods created. When she appeared on earth, each demon was determined to have her for himself. As a result fighting broke out among the demons and continued until all were killed. This, according to the myth, saved the world.

I have now learned that only one, the God-man, could save the world from the demons. For only Christ lived a sinless life. Only Christ died to pay the penalty for sin. Only Christ can forgive sins, and only through Him can a person be saved. Buddhism somehow lacked the power to help me, to forgive my sins, to save me. Gautama, the founder of Buddhism, was just a human, even though he had good intentions in his work and teachings.

As a girl in school I had heard about a savior who would appear, according to Buddhism, to save the righteous people. Also, at the same time this savior would cause the unrighteous to perish. It seems that sometime in the early history of Buddhism the people had begun looking forward to a savior.

The idea of a Buddhist savior may have actually come from the Bible, for the Bible is very clear that a Saviour would come to this world. Many prophecies in the Bible point forward to that Saviour-God. More than a thousand years before Buddhism even started, the Bible, in its early form, was predicting a God-man who would appear with the purpose of saving humanity. It is a historic fact that Jesus Christ did appear on earth more than 1,900 years ago. He healed the sick, resurrected the dead, and taught the people the ways of His kingdom. And before He left, He promised to return to gather the righteous and take them to His home.

In fact, the Bible also has scores of references to the second coming of Christ. It tells how He will come, when He will come, and the conditions of the world at the time of His coming. A study of these predictions and the condition the world is in today has convinced me that His return will be soon. As a result of getting to know Jesus Christ, my life has changed a great deal, for Christ has brought peace, security, and hope into the life of this refugee girl.

My life has also changed along material lines. May 1986 was graduation day for me. My nursing courses are behind me as well as my state board examination. Now I'm a registered nurse working at the Shady Grove Adventist Hospital in Gaithersburg, Maryland.

My brother Lim is enrolled at Columbia Union College in Takoma Park, Maryland, where he is training to become a minister in his newfound denomination. He hopes to someday return to Kampuchea to bring Jesus Christ and the hope of His soon return to his countrymen.

His decision to become a pastor came about through a

rather complicated process. As I mentioned earlier, he was first introduced to Adventism and baptized in the border camps in Thailand. After coming to America and graduating from high school, he began to think seriously about his lifework. During this time, some of his fellow students influenced him to think that true success is determined by the amount of money a person earns. Accepting this philosophy, Lim began to look for courses at college that would help him accomplish his materialistic goal. In pursuit of his objective, he studied hard and even went to California to further his education.

Although Lim had set his mind on being successful as most people understand success, he soon came to realize that something was missing. He was not satisfied or happy with his aim in life. It all seemed very hollow and meaningless. Then one day, while reflecting on his homeland, his thoughts focused on Father, who was well-educated and successful and who had made good money. Father filled some of the higher positions in the Cambodian government. As a result, his family had lived well and in a good house. Lim began to realize that one day Father had been a successful, well-paid government man and the next day a slave, driven from his home, and not knowing where his next meal would come from. The idea that money and position should be the real measure of success began to fade in his thinking, for it could all be swept away so quickly. Lim asked himself the question When money and position are gone, what does a person have left? The answer? Nothing!

Over against the success and tragedy of Father, Lim thought of Christian people today who have made Christ first in their life. They are not usually rich and are rarely looked upon as being successful as far as the world is concerned, but they are happy in their work. And their happiness does not depend on money or position, nor can it be taken away from them, because this happiness is centered in Jesus Christ. Lim learned that real happiness comes not from the possession of material things, but from the commitment to Jesus Christ.

In 1985, after Lim had returned to Maryland, he quietly

decided to turn his back on the idea that money and position meant success. While he was still weighing his options, still undecided about which line of work he should follow, another challenge came to him. Without knowing anything of Lim's struggles over his lifework, our American friend, Pastor Melvin Adams, asked him about his goals in life. Lim thought for a few moments, shrugged his shoulders, and admitted that he didn't know what he wanted to be. He guessed he was just going to school.

Our friend then suggested that he should consider training to become a gospel minister. He said there were thousands of Cambodians in the United States, and, as far as he knew, there were no Seventh-day Adventist Cambodian ministers for them. Looking even further ahead, he suggested that the time might come when Lim could go back to Cambodia and bring the good news about Jesus Christ to his countrymen.

Lim did not respond immediately to the suggestion, but without telling anyone of his plans, he began taking a new interest in his schoolwork. More than two years went by before our American friend received his answer. It came when he learned that Lim had enrolled at Columbia Union College for the purpose of studying for the ministry.

✾✾✾

In September of 1990, I had the privilege of returning to Kampuchea with my sister Letine, Pastor Melvin Adams, and 14 other individuals. Most of the members of our group were doctors, nurses, and dental personnel who were intent on helping the hundreds of orphans in the Phnom Penh area.

This first visit back to my homeland was filled with fear, tears, surprises, and strong emotions—fear of the Khmer Rouge, tears of joy as I met Mother's sister and other relatives, surprise at seeing the life and energy of Phnom Penh and emotions as the horrors and sufferings of the past were brought to life by The Museum of Genocidal Crime and the "Killing Fields" swept over me.

I did not intend to visit these last two places, but the group needed someone to translate for them. I agreed to go

134

and managed to control my emotions as we viewed the first few exhibits. At the Museum of Genocidal Crime, the picture gallery, where wall after wall is filled with photographs of the young men, women, and children who were tortured and killed, was too much for me. I began to see my sister, my brother, my niece, and my father in those pictures. Pastor Adams spotted my tears and suggested that I go outside to wait for the group.

They continued on. In the next two schoolrooms, they found little stalls about three feet wide and five feet long, built of brick and with walls about six feet high. Each one had a chain anchored in the concrete floor. The other end of the chain was fastened to an iron ankle clamp so the prisoner could not move more than two feet in any direction. An old ammunition box served as their toilet. The windows had strong iron bars anchored in cement, and the porch was enclosed with several layers of barbed wire.

In these little cubicles, prisoners had to write their confessions. If the confession did not satisfy the examiner, the inmate was scheduled for more torture to help activate the memory. One man was known to have rewritten his confession seven times, with severe periods of torture between each writing.

The tortures used at Tuol Sleng, S-21, included many of those I have already mentioned along with others such as: slowly cutting the end of people's fingers off, with a pair of pliers pulling the nipples out of the breasts of women, half-drowning individuals, whipping nude persons until they were almost unconscious, hanging people by the arms until they fainted then dunking them in water to revive them, slowing forcing a small steel bar into the back of the skull, turning a poisonous insect loose on nude bodies, and tying the hands of prisoners over their heads and down their backs toward their feet, then pulling the feet and hands together very tightly. While the nude man or woman was in this rigid position, the tormentors would slowly cut their chest/breasts and throat with a sharp blade.

Those who survived the torture in S-21 were sentenced to

death for their confessed "crimes" against the government, then sent 15 kilometers out of Phnom Penh to Choeung Ek, better known as the "killing fields." There they were crammed into a small building to wait their turn in the execution schedule.

At the "killing fields" more torture took place. Mothers with small children and babies were marched over to a pit near a large tree. Their clothes were taken from them, then soldiers wrenched the babies from their arms. One at a time the helpless, sobbing mothers were forced to watch while a soldier threw their baby into the air as another soldier tried to shoot the infant before it hit the ground. If they missed, the baby was severely injured by the fall. A soldier usually finished off the little one by banging its head against the trunk of the large tree and throwing the body into the grave. The mother was then struck on the back of the neck with a club and pushed into the grave. Other mothers were stripped, then forced to watch as their older children were picked up by their feet and banged against the tree before being thrown into the mass grave. Some prisoners were beheaded; still others killed by an ax.

More than 20,000 men, women, and children were tortured in my old high school, then killed and buried in the mass graves of the "killing fields." Most of the victims were young people. Many were members of the Khmer Rouge who had in some way offended the leadership and as punishment were tortured and killed. Today, a memorial containing 8,985 skulls found in the mass graves stands on these grounds, reminding the nation and all visitors of the demonic tortures that took place in Kampuchea between 1975 and 1979.

My visit back to my homeland was both a privilege and an ordeal.

❧

Without the open arms and help of the United States, I would still be deprived of my freedom and living in poverty. I'm indebted to the people of this country for giving me a second chance. It's impossible ever to repay this debt, but I'm determined to be a good American citizen, one who will make Americans thankful they invested in me.

During January of 1985, the Vietnamese army was driving Cambodian resistant groups into Thailand. The newspaper pictures of these events showed Cambodian people fleeing before the army. These pictures triggered my memory. All of a sudden I felt as though I were there again, fleeing for my life. My heart pounded as memories of suffering and hunger flooded my mind.

It's impossible to forget the horrors of the past. The merciless torture, the constant killings, are often dredged up by my subconscious in nightmares that vividly bring the past into the present. These graphic reruns resurrect scenes of the terrible hunger and thirst I endured, the time I watched Father walk away never to return, and that occasion when the American immigration official rejected my request to immigrate to the United States. These horrifying memories are slowly being buried as each month slips into history, but many of them still slip by my best efforts to forget, and past atrocities seem as though they took place only yesterday.

I'm proud of my homeland and proud to be a Cambodian. But because of the Khmer Rouge, unpleasant images cloud my memories. Many of my immediate and extended family are no longer with us. Scattered around my homeland are many unmarked graves of family members. In most cases their location is not known, but the memories of these loved ones are securely fixed in my mind.

My older sister, Sour Ly, lost her husband because of the Khmer Rouge. Bun Thuon Lok was in the Cambodian army when the Khmer Rouge took over the country. He has not been seen or heard from since and is presumed dead.

Sour Ly wanted to travel with us when we left Veal Treng, but could not because her baby was due at any time. We learned years later that the baby girl, whose name we never learned, died a few days after her birth and that Sour Ly and her mother-in-law were taken out and killed in 1977 by the Khmer Rouge because they were accused of having too much gold.

My older brother, Leng, was in the Cambodian Naval School when the Khmer Rouge took control. He has never been seen or heard from since and is presumed dead.

Most of Mother's family were killed. That included her brother, his wife, and their three sons, their daughter, and her five children. Also her sister and her sister's daughter, and her nine children.

My cousin, the one who lived across the street from our home in Phnom Penh, starved to death. The next day her oldest daughter also died of starvation. A short time later her little boy died from starvation as a sister held him in her arms.

My sister Nakry lost her husband when the village leader learned he was intending to escape. His three brothers were also killed about the same time.

My aunt died at the foot of the mountain when we were pushed back from Thailand. Many years later we learned that her son, who had moved to France, arrived on the Thai border looking for his mother just two days after she was forced to return to Kampuchea.

Someplace in the countryside of my homeland is a very special unmarked grave, the grave of Father, who was killed by the Khmer Rouge leader of our village.

Daily death could be seen, heard, and detected. It was on our every side. During the time that I almost starved to death, I could feel the grip of its icy cold fingers being tightened around my neck.

In the Bible, David talks about walking "through the valley of the shadow of death." Then with confidence he says, "I will fear no evil: for thou art with me" (Psalm 23:4). I walked through that cold, dark valley of the shadow of death but without the hope of the divine presence that David enjoyed.

Thousands upon thousands of my countrymen walked without hope through that same valley. Our stories are like the leaves of a tree, each one a little different but all with a common thread of hunger, slave labor, suffering, and death.

As I mentioned before, the new Kampuchean government

138

converted the Tuol Sleng high school into The Museum of Genocidal Crime, creating a showplace so the world can ponder the brutality of the Khmer Rouge. But I do not need such a place to understand the cruelty and suffering that the people of Kampuchea endured. I saw it with my own eyes. I heard it. I lived and suffered through it. That is the reason it means so much to me when someone says, "Between one and two million Cambodians died at the hands of the Khmer Rouge."

That statement is just words, abstract words, without meaning to most people. But to me it means my sister, my little niece, my cousins, my brother, my father. It means thousands upon thousands of mothers, some carrying unborn babies, others with babies in their arms, still others with three, four, or five little children, afraid, crying, clinging to their mother.

Those words bring back pictures of my friends, my neighbors, my schoolmates. I see people who laughed with me, people who cried with me, people who worked with me, people who dreamed with me, people who went to school and studied with me, people who loved me and hoped with me.

Those words stand for real, breathing, living human beings who had the same blood coursing through their veins as I have. But they are now all dead, having been forced to kneel at the edge of their grave, deliberately starved, tortured, overworked, clubbed to death, or denied needed medicine.

Now I am looking forward to the time when there will be no more mindless genocides in Cambodia or in any other country, to the time when all wars, sickness, sorrow, and death will be brought to an end and Christ returns to this earth to claim His own.

This is the end of my story, a sad one in many ways, but, on the other hand, a joyful one. I am well aware that I might have been one of the victims occupying an unmarked grave or that my skull might be on display in the "killing fields" today.

Before closing my story I want to express a wish. It may

sound strange at first, but with a little thought I think you will understand. It stems from my deep love for my father, his struggles to lead his family to freedom, and his untimely death.

Just before Father was killed he said to his friend, *"Tell my children to get revenge for me."* If it were possible, I would give the following message to Father.

Dear Father:

In spite of the cruel attempts of the Khmer Rouge and others to hold us in slavery, we escaped. They tried to blow out our little candles by using starvation. Some were extinguished, but father, they could not extinguish the flame of freedom you planted in our hearts.

In our new country we are receiving a good education. We have jobs, cars, a comfortable place to live, but most important, we are free. And father we don't have to work in the water and mud as slaves, nor run for our lives. We have enough to eat and we do not live in constant fear that someone will knock at our door in the night, taking us away, never again to return home.

Father, your last request was for your children to get revenge for your death. We have done as you requested. Today your family lives as free human beings, not like slaves. We have the satisfaction of escaping from the Khmer Rouge and the others that followed them.

Father, your death occurred on March 10, 1977. Twelve years later, again on March 10, but in the year 1989, I became a citizen of the United States of America. Now I'm free, father, and I'm living in a free nation. This is the best kind of revenge I know. I am sure, you would agree.

Love, your youngest daughter.
Vatha

PS

    Father, I often dream about you. When I wake up I wish my dreams were true and you were alive to enjoy the freedom we have found. Although I know my dreams will never come true in this life, I am sure I will see you again in the land of God. I'm eagerly looking forward to that day.

លោកប៉ាជាទីស្រឡាញ់,

ថ្មីបើពួកខ្មែរក្រហមបានប្រើអំណួចម្ចៅៗដោយ៥សាហាវឃង់
ឃ្នងដើម្បីបង្ខាំងយើងអោយរស់ក្នុងទាសភាពយ៉ាងណាក៍ដោយ
ក៏ត្រួសារយើងបានរត់គេចផុតពីនឹមជីវិតរបស់វាដែរ ។

ពួកវាចង់ពន្លត់ពន្លឺៗរៀនជីវិតយើងដោយប្រើការបង្អត់ៗបាយចំណី
អាហារ ។ បើទោះជាពួកវាបានសម្លាប់សមាជិកត្រួសារយើងខ្លះ
ក៏ដោយ ក៏ប៉ុន្តែវាមិនអាចពន្លត់ពន្លឺសេរីភាពដែលលោកប៉ា
បានបណ្ដុះក្នុងចិត្តពួកកូនបានទេ ។

ត្រួសារយើងបានមករស់នៅសហរដ្ឋអាមេរិក ហើយបានទទួល
នូវការរស់វិសិក្សាជាថ្មី ។ យើងមានការងារធ្វើ មានរថយន្តជិះ
មានផ្ទះសុខ៥ដុមនៅ និងជាពិសេសបំផុតគឺយើងមានសេរីភាព ។

ក្រៅពីនេះទៀត លោកប៉ាដឹងទេថាពួកយើងមិនចាំៗត្រូវធ្វើ
ការត្រាំទឹក ត្រាំភក់ៗជាំ ដូចទាសករ ឬក៏ត្រូវរត់គេចខ្លួនដើម្បីការពារ
ជីវិតឡើយ ។ យើងមានបាយចំណីៗញុំៗត្រប់គ្រាន់ៗពីកណ្ដាលមិន
មានខ្លះ ហើយយើងក៏បានជៀសផុតពីការរស់នៅទាំងភ័យខ្លាចរន្ធត់
មិនដឹងថាពេលណានិងមានគេមកគោះទ្វារហៅទៅទាំងយប់គ្មាន
ថ្ងៃត្រឡប់មកវិញៗឡើយ ។

លោកប៉ាអើយ, បណ្ដាំលោកប៉ាចុងក្រោយបានៗៗផ្ដៃៗៗ
អោយកូនលោកប៉ាសងសឹកជូន ។ កូនលោកប៉ាបានធ្វើតាម

142

បណ្ដាំហើយ ។ រហូតមកដល់ថ្ងៃនេះ កូនលោកគ្រាទាំងអស់
បានរស់នៅជាមនុស្សមានសេរីភាព ពុំមែនជាទាសករទៀតទេ ។
យើងបានទទួលនូវរលនូវផលល្អអំពីការកេ្សៀសខ្លួនពីនិរ្ទេសក្រហមនិង
ពួកបរិវារ ។ កូនទាំងអស់បានមករស់នៅក្នុងទឹកដីដែលមាន
សេរីភាពហើយ ។ យើងជាមនុស្សមានសេរីភាព ។

លោកគ្រា, លោកបានចែកឋានទៅនៅថ្ងៃទី ១០ ខែមិនាឆ្នាំ
១៩៣៣ ។ ១២ឆ្នាំកន្លងមក គឺនៅថ្ងៃទី១០ ខែមិនាឆ្នាំ ១៩៨៨
កូនបានចូលជាសញ្ជាតិអាមេរិកាំងរស់ដោយមានសេរីភាពនៅ
សហរដ្ឋអាមេរិក ។ នេះជាការសងសឹកដ៏ប្រសើរបំផុត ហើយកូន
យល់ច្បាស់ថា លោកគ្រាប្រកដជាយល់ព្រមនឹងការសងសឹកនេះជា
មិនខាន ។

ពីកូនស្រីពៅលោកគ្រា

វិណ្ណា

សេចក្ដីបន្ថែម

លោកគ្រា, កូនតែងតែសុបិនឃើញលោកគ្រាជានិច្ច ។ ពេល
កូនភ្ញាក់ដឹងខ្លួនឡើង កូនចង់អោយការសុបិនរបស់កូនក្លាយជាការ
ពិត ថាលោកគ្រានៅមានជីវិតបានមកសប្បាយរីករាយនឹងសេរីភាព
ដែលយើងបានរកឃើញនេះ ។

143

ថ្វីបើកូនដឹងថាការសុបិនរបស់កូនមិនអាចក្លាយជាការពិតបាន
ក្នុងជាតិនេះក៏ដោយ ក៏ប៉ុន្តែកូនយល់ប្រកដថាកូននឹងបានជួប
លោកម្ចាស់វិញនៅក្នុងដែនដីរបស់ព្រះជាម្ចាស់ ។ កូនរង់ចាំទំនឹងដល់
ថ្ងៃមួយនោះជានិច្ច ។